THE
CONTENT CODE

SIX ESSENTIAL STRATEGIES FOR IGNITING YOUR CONTENT, YOUR MARKETING, AND YOUR BUSINESS

MARK W. SCHAEFER

This book was produced in part through the generous patronage of Dell Inc. and gShift. Please support the sponsors who made the book possible.

This publication is designed to provide accurate and authoritative information in regard to the subject matter covered. It is sold with the understanding that neither the author nor the publisher is engaged in rendering legal, accounting, or other professional service. If legal advice or other expert assistance is required, the services of a competent professional person should be sought.
  - From a *Declaration of Principles jointly adopted by a Committee of the American Bar Association and a Committee of Publishers.*

Schaefer Marketing Solutions
www.businessesGROW.com
First Edition: March 2015
Publisher is not responsible for websites (or their content) that are not owned by the publisher.

Cover, Interior Layout and Design by Sarah Mason
www.uncommonlysocial.com

Library of Congress Cataloging-in-Publication Data
Schaefer, Mark W.
The Content Code: Six essential strategies to ignite your content, your marketing, and your business
Mark W. Schaefer - 1st ed.
ISBN-10: 0692372334

For my Alpha Audience. We create content but content also creates us. This is for those who read, think, and grow with me each day.

Other Books by Mark W. Schaefer

The Tao of Twitter
Return on Influence
Born to Blog (with Stanford Smith)
Social Media Explained

Contents

Introduction

E ach time I've written a book, I've tried to solve a problem and answer an important and complex question on the mind of my customers, my students, and my friends in the business world. My previous books have provided answers to questions like ...

Can you help me figure out Twitter?
Social media is overwhelming ... where do I start?
How do I begin and sustain a blog that actually helps my organization?
How do I become significant—perhaps even powerful and successful—on the web?

So far, so good. As long as I encounter big questions that require more than a blog post to answer, I suppose I will keep writing books. Here's the question at the heart of The Content Code:

> I'm a professional marketer working as hard as I can. I'm producing content, engaging on social media, and spinning right along with the revolving door of every digital marketing innovation and new platform. Why is my business not getting anywhere?

Here's the short answer: Because you're living in yesterday's world.

The persistent myth that surrounds much of marketing today is that content is king. And if you can just produce enough of this scintillating, ripped-from-the-headlines, epic and amazing stuff ... dripping with keywords, stuffed to the headlines with relevance, decorated with Pinterest-worthy graphics and videos, and podcasts and listicles ... you'll win.

We're stuck with a misconception that the most worthy content rises to the top, scorching the search rankings, and becoming a dazzling beacon for eager customers. And at one point, that was probably true. Early in the web's history, the balance between the content available online and our capacity to consume it was grossly out of balance. We were insatiable consumers, spending hours discovering the new information sources coming at us on the emerging World Wide Web.

But the balance has shifted. Dramatically.

Every company, agency, club, university, non-profit organization, and 13-year-old kid hoping to break out as the next Katy Perry is pumping out content. Nearly everyone with access to the Internet has joined the content creation party. Selfies. Videos. Love poems. Songs. Infographics. Grumpy Cat.

As you look at the future of this business landscape, there is no single trend that will have a more profound impact on how you market, where you market, and to whom you market than this overwhelming and uncontainable force of digital information density.

Of course, if you're currently working in marketing, PR, advertising, customer service, or sales, you already know that. The real question is, what do you do about it?

Answering that question has become my obsession. Are we just going to let this tsunami of content take us under? Do we play by Facebook's rules and hand over our money so we can reach our own hard-earned fans with our content? Do we just sit by and watch our great work become a de-valued commodity?

No. We need answers and ideas. We need alternatives. And that's why we're here. This is a book about hope, about breaking through this menacing wall of noise, and winning at marketing now—beyond content, beyond social media, beyond search engine optimization (if such a thing even exists any more). The Content Code starts where your current content marketing plan ends, for as you'll find out, creating another blog post or video is probably the least of your worries.

Creating great content is not the finish line. It's the starting line.

The imperative for your organization today is to unlock your content, unleash it, ignite it, and somehow convert it to measurable business value within this shrill world of overwhelming information.

I've spent the last year studying this essential concept of *content ignition*, and it has changed me. There is a science and psychology behind the act of sharing content that is awe-inspiring and beautiful and mesmerizing. People share content for hundreds of reasons, but there is a uniform process behind it inexorably linked to self-image, caring for others, and even compassion for an author or brand. It's an astonishingly intimate experience, a precious symbol of trust and communion with our content that I had never considered before.

I've also discovered that there is indeed a launch code for digital marketing success, a complex cocktail far beyond mere "promotion." It's a program that can nudge content to the top, help it become discovered, and unlock remarkable new economic value from the investment made in wonderful posts, pictures, podcasts, and other elements of marketing communications.

While most marketers have understandably had their heads down producing content and building their audience, it's time to look up again and see that we need to build a third competency – an ignition plan.

The new priority of content transmission is a combination of art, science, and maybe even a little mathematical magic that includes these six factors of The Content Code:

- Brand development
- Audience and Influencers
- Distribution, Advertising, Promotion, and SEO
- Authority
- Shareability embedded into each piece of content
- Social proof and social signals

The beauty of The Content Code is that it's accessible to anyone and businesses of any size. Whether you have a little time for marketing each week, or you can dedicate full-time resources to content ignition (and this is beginning to occur), this book is filled with hundreds of ideas that will help you triumph in the chaotic information marketplace today.

The future is more than copy writing. The future of marketing is copy igniting.

So let's get to it. Let's discover The Content Code.

CHAPTER ONE

The Ignition Switch

"Change before you have to."
– Jack Welch

Life used to be so straightforward for marketers.

Even 20 years ago, our options were limited. Advertise on TV, radio or print. Maybe throw in some billboards, PR, and trade shows for good measure. Those were the marketing channels in a nutshell. That's where marketers maneuvered, every week, every month, and every annual budget cycle ... with few exceptions.

Today, the marketing platform options are changing by the day ... and so are the rules of engagement! Let me explain what I mean.

Let's take a quick examination of the evolution of just one popular social media platform, Twitter. Twitter was founded in 2006. Within a few months, it became a beloved platform for communication in short bursts of 140 characters. But very rapidly, Twitter transformed dramatically—not necessarily because of any grand strategic business plan, but because businesses and faithful fans discovered so many remarkable and useful new ways to use it.

- The ubiquitous hashtag was first used at a tech conference in 2007. Slowly it caught on and is now the preferred method of promoting, discovering, and organizing content. Twitter (the company) had nothing to do with this transformational innovation.
- Many marketers consider Twitter the greatest source of real-time research ever created. Some businesses are using advanced search strategies so effectively to grow their businesses that it has replaced advertising.
- Twitter chats, another "user" invention, have become big business. A cult of self-made Twitter chat stars are making a decent income from sponsored chats.
- Twitter has become the de facto "second screen" for TV viewing, amplifying content and advertisements to the point where tweet velocity is an important measurement in the traditional Nielsen television rating system.
- Tweets are now being used for political polling, for defining consumer sentiment, for creating detailed buyer personas, and even for the inspiration to write new television plotlines.
- One blogger counted more than 300 independent applications dedicated to helping you manage, measure, and engage on Twitter.

… and the list goes on and on. Rarely does a week go by when there isn't some significant, new Twitter-related innovation available for marketers. You could literally make a career out of studying nothing but Twitter.

Now, multiply that by every digital platform in the world and you'll start to feel a little dizzy! And while this feverish pace of change is something to reckon with, it's not even the biggest worry for marketers. There's another, more important, mega-trend impacting almost every marketing strategy, tactic, and innovation in our industry: Malignant information density.

In the beginning, there was ... not much

Sometime around 1987, I plugged my first laptop computer into a wall phone socket and dialed up an Internet connection through AOL.

Do you remember that buzz-screech-hiss sound of a dial-up connection? That was the sound of excitement! I vividly recall downloading my first photo of a galaxy from the NASA site and calling to my wife and children to witness this miracle. A color photograph through the phone line! In only 10 minutes of download time!

In hindsight, that seems pretty lame, doesn't it? But I tell this story to make an important point. In the early years of the web, interesting content was scarce and we had lots of time to wait for that download. Grasping all that has happened between that first buzz-screech-hiss and today is vital if you want to understand the significance of The Content Code.

Back then, the seemingly astonishing ability to access a single piece of digital content was a thrill. We were starved for content and stared with wonder at anything we could obtain through this new electronic conduit.

Fast forward to 2009, the year I became a serious content creator. At that point, the web was still a relatively uncrowded content space. There were roughly one-third as many bloggers as there are now ... and even fewer podcast producers, video-makers, Pinterest pinners, Facebook posters, and Instagram photographers.

The social media/content model for a personal or business brand was easy: Create great content, spend a little effort on search engine optimization and promotion, and build your business when people found your goods and services through Google.

Those days are coming to an end, and as you're about to see, it's a pretty predictable revolution.

The third digital revolution

So far, there have been three distinct phases of digital marketing. These upheavals haven't replaced each other, but rather have built upon progress and moved us forward.

The first digital revolution occurred at the dawn of the web in the late 1990s when companies like AOL, Netscape, and Prodigy shook up the nascent Internet. Your business priority was simply getting out there and establishing a website. So the dawn of the Internet created a business focus on PRESENCE.

Once you had a site, it needed to be found. Enabled by companies like Alta Vista and ultimately Google, by the late 1990s your business priority turned to search engine optimization (and a $30 billion industry was created!). An emphasis on DISCOVERY was the priority for the second digital revolution.

Today, we're firmly in the third digital revolution, which has been enabled by social media and mobile technology. Your business goal in this phase is UTILITY—to help and serve people at their point of need, whether they're looking for a movie review, the best price on a laptop, or product information at the point of sale in a retail store. (And oh yes, there's a fourth revolution in sight, but you'll have to wait for Chapter 11 for that!)

As each phase progressed into the next, life became more difficult for marketers. If you were a pioneer and had an early website during the first revolution, you had an advantage until your competitors caught on. Likewise, if you were the first to crack the code on SEO in the second phase, Oh Happy Day! You led the search results as long as your competitors lagged behind. If they figured it out, once again it became more difficult, and expensive, to compete.

Today, the world has become more difficult for digital marketers because your competitors have also figured out they need to be fueling their helpful Internet presence with content. If you were first and dominant in your niche, good news, good news, good news! But if the niche is filling up, you're probably discovering a business state I characterize as Content Shock.

Let's unpack that idea a little because it represents the marketing problem at hand: *There is just too much content and too precious little time for people to consume it. How does that affect your business strategy?*

Content Shock rises

The content/social media/mobile revolution is entering a mature phase. The factors impacting your ability to cut through and be noticed—namely the amount of content available and our capacity to consume it—are in transition.

Of course the volume of free content is exploding at a ridiculous rate. There are many forecasts out there, but most center around a 500 percent estimated increase in the amount of information on the web between 2015 and 2020. If you can imagine the vastness of the web today … well, pretty soon we're going to have *five times that!* And some think that number is low, projecting as much as a staggering 1,000 percent increase in information density in that timeframe!

Do you think it might be just a little harder to stand out in the next few years?

But wait. Won't a lot of this information be coming from all of these connected sensors you hear about—the Internet of Things, where the roads are talking to the trucks and the trucks are tuned to your refrigerator so the store knows you need more beer? Or something like that.

No. Experts believe about 75 percent of the information increase will come from brands and individuals. All those selfies and cat pictures have to go somewhere, right? And they all compete for attention. Nearly every person on earth is becoming his or her own personal broadcast channel. This is a wonderful thing for consumers but one daunting wall of noise to cut through for a brand message.

The consumption side

Here's the good news: Every time there has been a technological breakthrough, the amount of content people consume gets a lift.

For centuries, all we had was newspapers and printed books. Then radio came along around 1920 and the time spent consuming content every day doubled from about two hours to four hours. Television, the Internet, and digital gaming all captured more attention, at the expense of outdoor and family activities. By 2011 Americans were consuming more than eight hours of content per day, according to Nielsen and other sources.[1]

The rapid perpetuation of mobile devices put a rocket behind content consumption once again because now we could consume our favorite pictures of Grumpy Cat, movie reviews, and YouTube videos from a train, a store, even in the middle of a cornfield if the mood struck.

Because of the mobile revolution, by 2014 the amount of content consumed had been propelled upward by another two full hours a day. Today, adults in the Western World consume content an average of 10 hours a day!

There is no person reading this book, and no person you have ever known, who has lived in a world where the amount of content consumed is *not* going up. How much higher can it go? 11 hours per day? 13? 14?

I don't know. Nobody knows. Some gamers already consume content 18 hours a day or more in one sitting. Is that our future? Sleep, consume, sleep, consume? The point is, we're approaching a physiological limit to content consumption.

This intersection of finite content consumption and the explosion of content availability is creating a marketing industry tremor I characterize as Content Shock.[2] In a scenario in which content supply is exponentially increasing while content demand remains flat, you have to work a lot harder just to preserve the same amount of "mindshare" you have with your customers today. And that scenario is exactly what is happening.

The evaporation of content marketing as we know it

Here's an example of what many businesses are experiencing in the Content Shock age. A mid-sized sporting goods company in America's Pacific Northwest had carved out a small, profitable niche and served an international group of customers, by following a classic social media marketing playbook:

- They were consistently creating a variety of helpful, high quality content pieces, many of them featuring customer stories.
- They reached out to popular athletes using their products and featured their adventures, stories, and videos.
- They actively engaged with their audience on Twitter, YouTube, and Facebook and had at least doubled their online audience for three consecutive years.
- They had invested in more content creation every year and had even hired their first full-time community manager, an extraordinary commitment for the small company with just 17 employees.

Despite their well-conceived marketing effort, their organic reach on Facebook (the number of people who see their content without advertising support) had declined 90 percent in nine months!

How did this happen?

A few years ago, if you did a reasonably good job with your content and engagement, you could expect that Facebook would "show" your post to about 30 percent of the people who follow you. Although this success rate varies a lot by industry, organic reach has declined in a cataclysmic freefall since 2011 to the point where it is near zero for most businesses, including my customer.

Why? Facebook's explanation is that there is an excessive amount of content. An average Facebook user can see nearly 2,000 stories in their daily newsfeed. That is far too much to consume, so the company uses an algorithm called EdgeRank to sharply edit what shows through to your customers.

For a small business that has depended on Facebook to connect with customers—and there are a lot of them—there are seemingly only two choices: 1) Spend even more money on producing high- quality content, hoping it might squeak through to a customer's news feed, or 2) Pay Facebook to promote or boost the post. Either way, competing at this new level comes with a cost.

But even this strategy of throwing money at the problem is backfiring for many. As more people seek to buy a limited number of Facebook ads, the ad prices are rising, pushing the price out of reach for many small businesses. And even if you can afford to advertise, research shows[3] that users are now blind to sponsored, branded content on Facebook. Given the repetitive and typical billboard-style/interruptive/insipient na-ture of the content it's not surprising.

And that is Content Shock in action.

This isn't just a consumer goods problem or a Facebook problem. One study concluded that between 60-70 percent of the content on a B2B company website is unseen.[4] The prob-lem exists in every digital channel. Information density is like a blacksmith's hammer pounding down on our marketing pro-grams, forging new ideas and strategies and pummeling the old ways of doing business. It's time for something new.

Implications of information density

I believe there are other, less obvious implications of this trend.

1. Deep pockets have an advantage. As each new media channel emerges, it's originally fueled by crude "local" content, but the eventual winners are the content creators with the deepest pockets. When television started, the airwaves were filled with local programming (sort of like the bloggers of their day!). All the cooking shows, game shows, and variety shows used local talent. Today, corporations have taken over and there is virtually no "local" content left on TV.

Years ago, the most popular YouTube videos were locally produced home movies. Today, the most-viewed videos are dominated by big brands and slickly-produced films and music videos.

Even with Facebook, the great equalizer of the social media world, the expense of promoting content goes up as advertising inventory goes down. Over time, low-budget content producers will be edged out of the consumer mindshare if they don't find new ways forward.

Going back to my sporting goods example, if the company's competitor had more financial resources to pay for its content to get through Facebook, the channel would eventually be closed off to my friends. This wasn't even a consideration a few years ago when the best content was sure to win.

2. Entry barriers become too high for some to compete. The deep pockets trend appears in even the smallest market niches. The companies that can overwhelm the market with content can effectively raise the entry hurdles for competitors and maybe even block them out of key search results entirely. Essentially, winning marketers *create* Content Shock for their competitors!

So the second implication of this trend is that barriers to successful content marketing will become high, perhaps impossibly high, for some businesses.

3. Information density is an engine for innovation.

Here's the magic of the entrepreneurial economy. When something isn't working anymore, someone will find something better to replace it! The information density hammer will forge new content forms and niche platforms that will expose new opportunities for early adopters and innovators.

The challenges at hand might seem difficult, but this is an era of infinite opportunity. You need to be clear-eyed and rational, developing your strategies based on what *is,* not what you *wish* things to be. How and when the Content Shock comes will vary greatly by business, by industry, by a lot of factors. For some, it might be years away; for others like the sporting goods company, it's happening now.

In the history of marketing, there have always been new frontiers enabled by technological breakthroughs and the visionaries who act first. What's the next area of innovation to pioneer when the implications of Content Shock become unbearable?

The Content Code is one of the answers to that question.

This book starts where great content ends. There are enough books out there touting the need for amazing content. That's a given. But epic content simply earns a seat at the table today. The real power only comes to those who can create content that connects, engages, and moves through the network through social sharing.

Research firm eMarketer reports that 83 percent of brand marketers view *social sharing* as the primary benefit of social media[5] because 70 percent of consumers say they are more likely to make a purchase based on a friend's social media updates.

That's a powerful number, which is why it's somewhat mystifying that nearly all the marketing industry dialogue has focused on creating more content, creating content more efficiently, automating content, and finding ways to measure content. But as the eMarketer study shows, brand power isn't coming through content. It's coming from content *transmitted by our trusted friends.*

Content marketing may start with writing, but the money is made by IGNITING.

And that's where the conversation needs to be now. The most breathtaking content that remains undiscovered on a website has no more value to a business than a manuscript for a sensational novel that is locked away from sight in a dark, cold vault.

Why content isn't king

Here's something that is obvious to any person trying to carve a successful path in marketing today: Content marketing has little to do with content anymore.

Allow me to tell a funny story about how this revelation dawned on me.

My early days as a blogger were fraught with frustration. I believed my content was as good as anybody else's, but it wasn't attracting any reader engagement, let alone business opportunities. Mine was a quiet, lonely little corner of the web.

I was following the Big Blogger Best Practices by publishing consistently, connecting with others to form a community, and writing posts that were thought-provoking and original. Yet, my content languished.

In my blog's second year, I was beginning to find my voice. I confidently wrote original posts on influence marketing, electrifying digital trends, and new marketing insights. And still, my ideas were met with stone-cold silence.

At the same time that I was churning out these meaningful posts, Chris Brogan, an extremely popular entrepreneur who blogs about marketing and business issues, published a post that was exactly 37 words long. For your edification and entertainment, here's his entire post:

> "If you're going to speak to people, speak TO (or even better WITH) them. Don't look at your slides, read your slides, and tell me what's on your slides. I know how to read. Stop it. Okay?"

That's the whole thing.

What made this post remarkable is that it received nearly 400 social shares, or more than *10 shares per word.* It received more than 50 unique reader comments—more reactions than the total words in the post! The comments were uniformly enthusiastic and even included descriptions like "brilliant!!!!" and "awesome."

I'm going to go *way* out on a limb and say it was not an epic post. In fact, it's pretty standard presentation advice that has been delivered since the days of flip charts and transparencies. If someone gave you this advice in a company training program, you might roll your eyes and yawn. I'll even hypothesize that Chris would admit his post doesn't teeter into a category of "brilliant" posts!

Years later Chris and I would become friends, but at that moment I felt resentful and angry that a dull 37-word post received more web traffic than my blog had received *in an entire year.*

What was going on here?

If the Internet is the great equalizer, a meritocracy where all good work is rewarded, and if great content always rises to the top like the social media gurus were telling me, why did this post ignite and mine didn't? I hypothesized at the time that if Chris wrote a post titled "I'm feeling a little gassy today" it would have been tweeted 300 times. I actually encouraged him to do this as an experiment but alas, he declined. The world is poorer for it.

How did Chris get to a place where just about any content he published lit up the web like he'd struck a match in a fireworks store? Did content marketing success have *anything* to do with his content … or did he possess some personal magic that I didn't understand? Was there a secret content launch code I was missing?

I wanted to figure this out! And honestly, if I was going to succeed as a marketing consultant and teacher, I *had* to figure this out.

One of my (few) blog readers reflected my own exasperation in a blog comment at the time: "The people who claim great content always rises to the top are already in a dominant market position. For those of us starting out, trying to scratch out a presence, it seems that no amount of work gets us noticed. How do we crack this code?"

Indeed. What IS THE CODE?

Others were beginning to uncover clues to this formula, too. My friend Marcela DeVivo, an SEO specialist, business owner, and blogger in Los Angeles, expressed a similar frustration with her content failures:

> "I wrote a post about social media audits and published it on my blog. It received no comments or social activity AT ALL. I later submitted the exact same piece to the Social Media Today website. It was tweeted hundreds of times and I also had some great responses across the blogosphere.
>
> So much for great content. It's the exact same article, but since my blog doesn't have authority or community, it wouldn't have been found or read regardless of the quality of my work.
>
> I think at this point the focus has to move from content creation toward the idea of building community, developing strategies to distribute the content, and marketing to promote every piece."

Marcela hit on some more suspicions that point to the elusive Content Code: *Regardless of quality, content marketing success must also include community, distribution, and promotion.*

The Mirabeau miracle

Consider one more example that points to the secrets to content marketing success in an information dense world.

A few years ago, I was approached by a friendly fellow named Stephen Cronk for help on a new marketing strategy. Here's a summary of his story:

- He left his corporate job in London and moved his family to the Provence region of France.
- In the teeth of a recession and with no previous winemaking experience, he started a new winery called Mirabeau.
- He had 600 established competitors—and that was just in Provence!

This was a tough assignment, but I do love a challenge, and most important, I believed in Stephen. He possessed an excellent business mind, an urgency to learn, and a great sense of storytelling. I had to say yes!

Our first step was to determine where he could maneuver in a highly saturated, low-growth market. We couldn't afford to be a "me too." We conducted a complete market and competitive analysis and discovered that among the hundreds of wineries in his region, none of them had a meaningful digital marketing presence. At the same time, his potential retail customers were trying to gain a foothold in the social media space. In this intersection, we found our opportunity.

We had to scale a content marketing effort quickly and decided that Stephen's primary source would be video. He was a natural on camera, and the lush and ancient countryside of Provence provided an ideal backdrop to explore wine making, food, history, art, and the local color.

Stephen consistently documented his wine-making journey in a very human and entertaining way. He talked about a labeling crisis that almost crushed his business. He created entertaining videos about the ridiculous paperwork he faced from the French government, what it was like to attend an international wine-tasting competition, and how the grapes were harvested in the early morning sunlight. He created stories about his village, his pets, and his family. He shared his anguish as he knelt beside grape vines decimated by a 13-minute hail storm. He captured the pure joy of his children dancing while on a family vacation.

He was putting a human and modern face to a stodgy, traditional business.

In addition to producing content, we also had a network strategy and continuously worked on building a wine-loving audience that was passionate about his product and the stories from his little family business. As his audience and engagement multiplied, Stephen was able to share this data with huge wine retailers to prove a point of differentiation. No winemaker in the region had the presence and audience that the upstart Mirabeau had. The strategy worked, and the orders started coming in.

Stephen followed our strategy to dominate this unsaturated content niche and his progress was steady. But on his 222nd video, Stephen found the gold at the end of the rainbow. In just 29 seconds, he demonstrated how to open a wine bottle with only his shoe.[6] That video has now attracted well over 9 million views ... one of the greatest small business video success stories in the history of the web!

The viral attention gave a significant lift to all the content on the site. Because Stephen had worked so long and hard to provide entertaining videos, the viral visitors stuck around to see what else he had for them. Since the "shoe video," the winery's "About Mirabeau" video on its YouTube channel has received more than 10,000 new views. Facebook, Twitter, Pinterest accounts, and newsletter subscriptions have had massive gains.

The tiny winery received immense media attention from both the mainstream press and wine industry bloggers who marveled at Stephen's authentic and human storytelling:

> "The lesson wannabe Cronks should take on board is that throughout his video-creating efforts, he has never sought to use the clips to directly promote his wines or the brand. They are all intended to be interesting in their own terms and often contain no direct reference to the brand at all. People who watch them are merely invited to visit the website if they want to know more."

The clues emerge

What can you learn from this? Were there elements of a standard Content Code embedded in this inspiring success? If this humble winemaker went viral with his shoe video, can you, too?

There's no way to predict whether something will go viral, but Stephen's video provides more clues to the Content Code: The video was optimistic, entertaining, and practical, and as the wine blogger noted, it was characteristically "human." It also hit big only after Stephen had spent nearly three years honing his storytelling skills and building an extremely loyal audience that was able to start the content ignition process.

Is it possible to embed some of these elements in your content to tip the balance in your favor? Is there a science behind making content shareable?

From these three diverse case studies we are collecting some clues that point to a unifying Content Code.

There are four primary uses of social media for business: Monitoring and research, responding to customers, amplifying messages, and establishing thought leadership. The last two are closely linked to the idea that your content actually is received by somebody on the other end! So in order for most social media marketing to work, social sharing, or *transmission*, is essential.

Let's take it to the next level and specifically define the six key elements of the Content Code. Excited? Me too!

CHAPTER TWO

Structure, Strategy, and the Content Code

"If it keeps on raining, levee's gonna break."
– Bob Dylan

T his chapter examines what your content marketing strategy needs to look like in this Formula One–fast digital world, and I introduce the specific elements of the Content Code that are unpacked throughout the rest of the book.

But to kick things off, I need to talk about soup.

"Soup?" you say. "I bought this book to learn about soup?"

Trust me. I need to bring out the broth to tell a little tale that illustrates how marketers must think about content and marketing strategy differently in this era of information density and hyper-competition.

My friend Robert runs a downtown restaurant that specializes in soup. He had the very bright idea to partner with a local car dealership to offer potential customers a free lunch of delicious soup every Thursday (SOUPER THURSDAY!). The car dealer figured the small cost of some good soup was an intelligent investment in customer acquisition. And he was right! Every Thursday his store was flooded with people seeking Robert's soup. Life was good.

But then a competing car dealership down the street woke up and realized the advantage of the free lunch offer. The competitor started offering sandwiches and salads head-to-head with Robert every Thursday. The competitor even threw in his wife's famous home-baked cookies for dessert!

Suddenly, Robert and his dealership partner saw Souper Thursday visits drop dramatically. Most customers abandoned his modest soup menu for the competitor's tastier offering. The dealership owner turned to Robert and said, "Look what's happening! The soup isn't working anymore. We need something bigger and better! Steaks! Lobster! A dessert buffet! Starting this week, you need to be making epic gourmet food!"

Now how was Robert going to do that? He had limited resources and a one-burner stove in his kitchen that could only handle soup! And would the escalation stop there? Was this a sustainable strategy?

The content arms race and the unsaturated niche

In this little parable, you can begin to see parallels to a saturated content environment. Attempting to be epic enough to succeed in a highly competitive environment comes at a cost. Similarly, as the content arms race heats up in a particular niche, it may not be a sustainable strategy for all businesses ... although customers certainly LOVE all the free stuff coming their way!

By the way, Robert the soup maker isn't out of the game. He can find new markets for his soup. He can look for new ways to deliver his soup. He can repackage his soup so people can consume it in new places. But one thing is clear: Whatever the strategy, in a highly competitive environment, the status quo is not good enough. If you're facing a possibility of content saturation in your market, you need to be thinking of ways to change the game.

Although the world is facing an incredible content glut, this doesn't necessarily mean doom and gloom for everyone. In many industries, there's no glut at all. Consumers are still starving for helpful new content to serve them. If you're in one of these niches, you probably don't have to worry about Content Shock for some time. In fact, your job is to *create it!*

Without the Content Code, the only sustainable content strategy has been to find an unsaturated niche and overwhelm the web with so much quality content that search engines discover only you. Effectively, you're creating Content Shock by crowding out your competitors. The strategy is this simple:

1. Find an unsaturated niche.
2. Consistently produce a volume of quality, helpful material aimed at a relevant audience (or persona).
3. Never stop producing content.

Dominating a niche early has extremely important long-term value because the search engines will continue to recognize and reward the authority your website accrues for a long time. One pioneering blogger told me that after dominating his niche with content for so long, he could probably remain at the top of most search engines for years ... even if he never wrote another blog post again.

The Content Saturation Index

Marcus Sheridan, an entrepreneur and content marketing thought leader, created a theoretical term to describe this condition -- "content saturation index."[1] While his social media drug of choice is blogging, his experience relates to any content form. He described in a post:

> "The more content an industry/niche has written about it, the harder it is for a blog to make headway and find success in that field. And when an industry has very little online content available to the masses, it can often be gobbled up within almost no time at all.

> "Let me give you an example of both extremes. In March of 2009, I started blogging for my swimming pool company. At the time, less than 20 percent of our website traffic was 'organic' (free through search). The rest came from PPC (Pay Per Click) and 'direct.' Within six months—and after blogging 2–3 times a week—there was a significant shift in our numbers and the organic traffic started to grow dramatically. It was also during this time we started to experience more leads and sales because of this newfound traffic.

> "Within 18 months, the blog had elevated the website to an elite status in the swimming pool industry ... This success also enabled us to cut all of our old-school advertising and go 100 percent 'all-in' with blogging/content marketing.

THE CONTENT CODE | 31

"None of this would have been possible had the Content Saturation Index of the swimming pool industry not been so low. In other words, because so many 'pool guys' had zero interest in producing great content on their websites to teach the masses, it left a field wide open for someone like me to come in and have a complete harvest.

"On the reverse side of the coin, let's take a look at my efforts to establish myself in the digital marketing space. In a field focused on blogging, marketing, and business tips, you can imagine just how much content is currently out there. The number of folks writing about this stuff is growing by the day, which is one reason why so many bloggers and businesses struggle to stand out in the fields of marketing, self-improvement, sales, etc.

"I started The Sales Lion blog in November of 2009. At the time, I naturally figured I'd just walk right in, just as I'd done in the swimming pool industry, and dominate. Boy was I wrong.

"For the first year, this blog grew very little. In fact, it really wasn't until I woke up and started working much harder on my networking that things finally picked up around the beginning of 2011. Luckily for me, I wasn't dependent on The Sales Lion to pay my bills during this time period; otherwise I would have gone broke."

How do you know whether your particular niche is actually saturated? Christopher Penn, an analytics expert and author of *The Marketing Blue Belt* provides an answer in this section: A free, but somewhat inaccurate method, and the expensive, accurate method.

Free, somewhat accurate method

Let's start with the basic, humble search engine, a decent place to begin building your Content Saturation Index. Open up a spreadsheet to keep track of things, or a pad and paper if you prefer analog solutions. Next, type in your industry and the word blog. Be specific. We'll use Marcus Sheridan's industry, swimming pools, as an example:

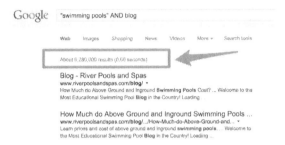

Wow – more than 8 million results. That's a lot of content out there about swimming pools. Content Shock has occurred for this niche. The space is saturated at the very top level of content. But let's dig deeper. What if there were a niche we could specialize in? How about saltwater swimming pools?

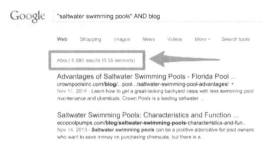

Only 8,680 results. This result is several orders of magnitude better for a more defined niche. There's opportunity there, if we're willing to specialize in it because the saltwater swimming pool space isn't saturated with content. Now repeat this search for a series of other possible niche topics that could represent potential markets for your business, such as in-ground swimming pools, fiberglass pools, concrete pools, above-ground swimming pools, and any other relevant term. Soon, you'll have a general sense of where you have the opportunity to maneuver.

Expensive, More Accurate

Many subscription social media and SEO tools can do an even better job of accurately assessing the content available in a specific time period. This is more valuable than the search engine result technique because you can see how fast a particular topic is accelerating toward content saturation.

Here is an example from the Sysomos MAP monitoring tool, examining just blogs by search topic for the last calendar year. "Swimming pools" is the dominant topic of content creation, while saltwater swimming pools represents a wide open market to establish a "share of voice."

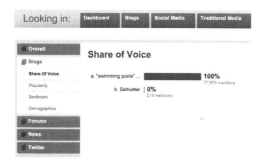

Sysomos MAP and other high-end monitoring tools can provide excellent estimates of just how much content has been created in your niche in a defined period of time. But then it's up to you to determine a strategy and whether you have the resources to actually create Content Shock for your competitors in a business niche.

Saturation Guidelines

So what constitutes "saturation?" As these examples show, the higher the information density in a niche, the more difficult it will be to create outstanding content that will shine through on its own without investment in distribution, promotion, and advertising. Here are rough guidelines outlined by Penn, using Google search results as an index for relative saturation levels.

- If there are fewer than 10,000 pages of returned search results, full speed ahead! There's an opportunity for you since there is low content density.
- Between 10,000 and 100,000 results, expect some resistance, but it's surmountable with minimal investment, exceptional content, and implementation of some of the Content Code factors covered in this book.
- If there are between 100,000 and 1 million search results, expect significant resistance. Competing through content alone will be difficult. Applying Content Code strategies might be the primary means of rising above this level of saturation.
- A result producing more than 1 million pages of content represents a thoroughly saturated niche. Unless the content becomes a product in its own right

through significant investment, Content Shock exists in this niche and is likely to bury even exceptional content creation efforts. In this situation, the Content Code strategies would be the only possibility of strategic leverage.

Examining the relative saturation in your niche is crucial to understanding how the Content Code formula will or will not work for your market. It's extremely difficult to unseat somebody in the search engine ranking if they have dominated a niche, even if you're doing great work. But it's not hopeless.

Of course the strategies in this book are going to work well in an environment where the content competition is still relatively low. If you're fortunate enough to already own an unsaturated content niche, chances are you'll dominate the search engine rankings too, and the Content Code will widen the gap between you and the laggards.

However, if you're behind in your market and you're feeling like it's "game over," the Content Code can provide you with an ignition strategy and an entirely new opportunity to maneuver.

Winning in the face of information overload

Let's take a look at how a content ignition strategy can work in even the most desperate marketing situations.

I was asked to provide a marketing strategy for a client in an extraordinarily difficult situation. The well-known global brand was entering a new market with high content saturation dominated by three established competitors. In terms of content marketing, one leading competitor had dominated every platform, every subject, and every content style to the point where trying to compete seemed hopeless.

The client called me in to do content marketing triage, and after a few months of intense research and deliberation, I presented three tactics to provide this company some room to maneuver.

1. Focus on sub-categories.

The competitor had overlooked new demographic subsets who were coming into the market and eager to use their products. When I did research on these segments, I found a wide open opportunity. The competitor had no content targeted to these personas. We set about dominating the under-served channels with amazing new content served up especially for them.

2. Explore different types of content.

YouTube first floated the idea[2] that different types of content, when combined together in an ideal mix, are extremely successful in building an engaged audience for the long-term. The three types of content are:

- **Hygiene content:** This is the content that serves the daily health of your audience. This content makes them aware of your brand and helps them connect to you when they need you most. This is the specific, short-form content that is most likely to turn up in organic search results. An example of hygiene content is a series of how-to videos from a do-it-yourself store like Home Depot.
- **Hub content:** While hygiene content might get somebody to your site, hub content is intended to

keep them there. This could be a series of articles about a more in-depth topic, or perhaps a serialized story, that makes people want to go down the rabbit hole and stay on your site. This could also be "evergreen" content that people seem to love and read month after month. An example of hub content is the addictive and thrilling adventure videos produced by Adidas Outdoor featuring daredevil athletes using their gear. Hub content lifts subscriptions to your content, spurs engagement, builds brand interest, and may even lead to brand loyalty.

- **Hero content:** Hero content is something brilliant, dramatic, and bold that transcends the normal day-to-day Internet offerings. This is the content that creates viral buzz. A famous example is the epic videos Nike created to celebrate the World Cup. The most recent one, "Winner Stays," playfully captures the schoolyard fantasy of young soccer players who morph into their favorite global stars. This type of content is difficult to produce. Nike was intentional in spending millions to create this hero content with the goal of creating massive brand awareness and dominating the conversation around the world's biggest sporting event. The video received 100 million views.

We'll be exploring these "3H's" of content and how they relate to social sharing in Chapter 8, but for now it's important to understand that each type of content plays a role in the overall brand-building plan. One way to carve a place for yourself is to create content in a category your competitors might be missing. In the specific case of my client battling three big competitors, we learned that there was an opening in the hygiene content category that would allow us to capture a niche that leads to search engine traffic.

3. Focus on social transmission.

Here's the mistake most companies make: They check the box on content and then forget about ignition. As I introduced in Chapter 1, content isn't effective if it doesn't *move*. People have to see it, engage with it, share it—or you're wasting your money. By putting the emphasis on exposing your content instead of simply producing more, more, more, you create a powerful new marketing competency in the information era.

This is where we're going to spend our time for the rest of this book. You'll become an expert on this complex cocktail of ideas and insights, promotion and production, audience and audacity ... that gets your content to explode through this wall of information density.

The economics of ignition

In addition to providing new strategic options, the six elements of the Content Code can provide measurable economic benefits in at least four ways:

1. You will realize exponential gains in the return on your initial investment in quality content.
2. You will find ways to produce new content more cost-effectively by building in data-based, high-probability success factors.
3. You will create a unique competitive advantage by establishing a core competency in content transmission.

(It's like running your marketing program on rocket fuel while your competitors are still trying to light a match.)

4. You will avoid advertising and promotional costs to the extent that you can increase brand awareness through more effective organic content transmission.

The six elements of the Content Code

We've established that great content is rarely enough to assure success. Great content is simply the table stakes needed to earn a seat at the table. I'm not going to cover tips and tricks about writing for the web or creating epic videos. Those topics have already been effectively covered in many other places. We're here to plow new ground.

So here is the starting line for this race: You need great content.

Let me repeat: You need great content. But then what?

This is where the Content Code takes over. Content that rises and is discovered through search is a mixture of art, science, and magic that includes these six factors:

- Brand development
- Audience and Influencers
- Distribution, Advertising, Promotion, and SEO
- Authority
- "Shareability" embedded into each piece of content
- Social proof and social signals

Now, if you're paying close attention—and I'm sure you are—the first letter of each piece of the Content Code spells out **BADASS**.

I consider this a giddy coincidence and perhaps the highlight of my professional career. I'm tempted to end the book right now as I'm sure there is nothing I can write that can ever top this. I bet you didn't see that coming did you? You should send me a selfie right now with the look of surprise and amazement on your face. #BadassSelfie

Okay, time to settle down. We must get back to the topic at hand, for this is a serious book for serious people. What does this BADASS thing really mean?

Provided you start with great content (did I already mention that?), if you commit to continuously working on these six factors you'll begin to crack the code. Although the six factors have been written about in bits and pieces by many talented experts (whom I call on to help tell the story), this is the first time the entire Content Code has been assembled in a cohesive way, in one book.

In the chapters that follow, we will dive into each of these factors in detail, but the overall recipe for how you execute your plan is up to you. You see, there's no simple strategy that fits everybody ...

- A business competing to sell discrete items in an eCommerce environment will want to emphasize brand building and search optimization.
- A lawyer, management consultant, or accountant will probably want to focus on establishing authority and a large, engaged audience consisting of consumers of their services.

- A company in a highly competitive international market may need to spend money on promotion and advertising to get their message through.
- An individual starting a blog might seek a true balance of all six factors but concentrate on writing highly shareable content and building a heroic personal brand that leads to fanatic supporters and business benefits.

So the best way to use this book is to take a dive into all six pools and see what fits for your particular situation. You don't necessarily need to work on all six factors to make progress. Pick out one or two that fit your business situation and capabilities, and you certainly will be better prepared for the future than your competitors! Most of the ideas in the book are accessible to companies big and small.

While the BADASS thing is awesome and perhaps a useful mnemonic device, I actually start the deep dive on this subject of content ignition with an "S"—shareability—because I believe it's vital enough that nearly every business, brand, or individual needs to work on it. Building shareability into your content may be the most important concept in the book. After all, what good is all that content if people won't share it?

CHAPTER THREE

Building Shareability into Your Content

"If an infographic is published and no one shares it, did it even exist?" – Brian Solis

Welcome to Chapter 3. This is one bold and sassy chapter. It's the barbecue sauce of book chapters. It's a chapter with a topic so gigantic, it takes two chapters to cover it all!

In this episode of The Content Code, we'll look at the fascinating reasons why people share content and how we can use that insight to ignite our own work. The next chapter continues the discussion of shareability with an astonishing list of practical tips and tricks you can start using right now.

The concept of shareability builds upon important tenets from the first two chapters of this book, so here's a quick review:

- Business results on the web don't come from content; they come from content that moves.
- Even if your content is great, there's no guarantee it will rise to the top in an increasingly competitive world.
- Exploding information density effectively negates many traditional marketing strategies and increases the cost to remain competitive.
- Implementing elements of the Content Code (BA-DASS) will give your content the best chance to cut through the noise and be heard.

The heart of the book, the first element of the Content Code, begins with a critically important idea of shareability, which is actively building the possibility for ignition into your content. I want to be clear that sharing is different than a "Like," a comment, or a "Plus 1." Content transmission is what you're after. Spreading the word. Building the buzz.

It may be true that most frequently shared posts also get a lot of Likes and comments, and there also many posts that are frequently Liked but barely shared. A leading reason that posts can be Liked but not shared is that a person may Like a post to support a political, theological, or philosophical view that may upset a general audience if it is transmitted broadly. We generally don't want to make people uncomfortable, so we don't always share.

Liking lightly bonds us with other likers of that thing. But when we share, we're virtually shouting, "I'm in this club and I want to show the world!" As you're about to see, this kind of commitment isn't necessarily easy to achieve.

Content that moves on the web may or may not have anything to do with quality, or even the content! Why do you tweet a link, post a video to Facebook, or email a link to your family and friends? Is it because somebody did a very, very good job with search engine optimization? Is it because the video has superb cinematography, or the writing in a blog post is scintillating? Perhaps ... but chances are the reason is more subtle ... and surprising.

Understanding *why* people choose to share content sheds light on how you can adjust your strategy and carve out a competitive edge by embedding shareability into everything you create. Think about content you recently shared. Why did you do it? Do any of these reasons ring true?

- It made you look cooler, smarter, funnier, or more relevant—providing you with a personal psychological benefit.
- The content struck some strong emotional chord. It made you laugh, cry, or otherwise feel something so profound it deserved to be shared with others.
- It's practical or timely. Sharing the content will help and inform your friends.
- You found a new idea and can't wait to be the first to share it.
- You feel deeply connected to the author and you want to support them.

- It represents an achievement. Maybe you or your company were mentioned in the content and it makes you feel good to show this representation of your status.

These are some of the reasons people might share content, and in this age of information density, you need to give your content every advantage you can by tapping into the psychology of sharing. This chapter will begin to deliver that edge for you and your business.

Before we dive headlong into some exciting ideas, it's important to remember that there's no one-size-fits-all solution for any business or content strategy. If your audience is into Kim Kardashian quotes and cat videos, then those content sources should be an important part of your ignition strategy. Also, keep in mind that a majority of the research presented in this book is U.S.-based (because that is where most of the research is occurring). So you need to be culturally sensitive to the unique needs of your region and target audience.

I provide sound advice based on the experience of experts and trusted research, but you should always apply critical thinking, your own data, and personal intuition about your customer needs to create a plan that is exactly right for you and your business.

Breaking through the wall

First, the bad news: In general, people don't want to share your content!

Research shows that people typically don't share content they're reading on the web, even "great" content.[1] For example, a large study of social transmission across millions of Twitter accounts revealed that the majority of users are passive information consumers and rarely forward content to their network.

In fact, an average Twitter user retweets only one in 318 content links they receive. Facebook reports that just one-half of one percent of those who see a Facebook post share it.[2] These sobering numbers suggest that actively finding and nurturing that miniscule number of the most active users is critical to spreading your information on the web.

The popularity of an individual or brand, the nature of the content, and the size of the audience alone are not accurate predictors that people will overcome this passivity and "click" to share.

Therefore, in order to become an effective content-igniter, you must not only create content and build an audience but also employ strategies to overcome user passivity and systematically find individuals predisposed to love and share the content you're creating. This is perhaps the *most overlooked imperative in digital marketing today.*

The psychology of sharing

There's a lot of hype about what makes content work in a way that people want to share it. Instead of buying into the hype, let's focus on reliable research that can provide accurate insight and even competitive advantage as you seek to overcome passivity and build shareability into every piece of content.

If there is any organization on earth that wants to attract page views, it's a newspaper, so let's pay attention to what one of the most important newspapers in the world has to say. *The*

New York Times [3] sponsored research that determined there are five powerful reasons people overcome apathy and share content:

- **To be useful.** The number one reason people share content is to bring valuable and entertaining content to others. More than 90 percent of study participants said they carefully consider how the information they share will be useful to the recipient.

- **To define ourselves to others.** Nearly 70 percent of participants said they share content to give people a better sense of who they are and what they care about. One respondent said, "I try to share information that will reinforce the image I'd like to present— thoughtful, reasoned, kind, interested, and passionate about certain things."

- **To grow and nourish relationships.** About 80 percent of participants share information online because it lets them stay connected to people they may not otherwise stay in touch with. A little over 70 percent share content to help connect them to new people who share common interests.

- **Self-fulfillment.** About 70 percent of participants share content because it allows them to feel more involved in the world. The act of getting positive feedback on shares makes people feel valued.

- **To get the word out about causes and brands.** More than 80 percent of participants said they share content to rally others around a cause, company, or idea they believe in.

As you read this list, it probably occurs to you that sharing content is a meaningful act, a very personal, intimate, and important gesture. It's not at all trivial.

The decision to share content is often a sign of a relationship. A relationship with the source, a relationship with a network...even a relationship between the person and the content! Igniting content is a symbol of kindness and caring and a reflection of who we are.

Pretty deep stuff.

One of my blog readers recently sent me this note:

> "Your blog has become part of my morning routine. I start my day with a cup of coffee and your latest blog post! I almost always share your posts with my friends because I feel like I know you. Your perspective aligns with my business values and I feel good about sharing your thoughts with others ... and even with family members."

There is a lot of rich insight in this brief message:

- My content has connected to her on an emotional level, and I've become part of the fabric of her life.
- Although I've never met this person or even spoken to her on the phone, she feels as if she knows me as a friend. She has built a kinship with me through my content alone.
- Sharing my content is an act of adding value to her friends. It enhances her self-view because my values reflect her values. And the bond created through my words is so strong that she feels comfortable making me part of her family communications at times.

I've built "shareability" into my content over time by nurturing a relationship of trust with the reader. I can't appeal to everyone, of course—there are people who unsubscribe to my blog all the time. But for those who do connect, they seem to connect deeply.

We'll explore some of these important emotional and brand-building imperatives in upcoming chapters, but for now let's dig a little more into the topic of embedding shareability into your content and the psychology of content ignition.

Sharing creates involved, smarter consumers

Sharing content isn't just about building "traffic." The act of sharing content actually helps consumers process your information better. A separate *New York Times* study[4] on why and how people share content found that:

- 73 percent of participants say they process information "more deeply, thoroughly, and thoughtfully" when they share it.
- 85 percent say reading content that other people share helps them understand and process information and events.
- 49 percent say sharing allows them to inform others of products they care about and potentially change opinions or encourage action.

Participants say the act of sharing content helps them remember products and information sources better and makes them more likely to use them. So if you create ideal conditions for content-sharing, you both build power for your brand and create new economic value by helping your consumers understand you and become authentic advocates for your products and ideas!

With this perspective, you begin to see that getting people to transmit your content through their network can't be reduced to SEO techniques or get-rich-quick schemes to drive massive traffic to your website. Shareability requires connection of some kind; your content must fill a need or perhaps even reflect on a trusted relationship.

The primal need

Sometimes, content goes viral due to luck. There are millions of cat videos. Why do a few become a hit? There are millions of kids singing songs on YouTube. Only a handful of them truly ignite. Who knows why?

I don't think you should build a business case around getting lucky. Instead, you need to look at some of the techniques you can apply over time to give your content the very best shot at transmission.

Most of the value created on the social web every day is non-economic. Do your friends wile away their hours on Facebook to be more profitable? Of course not.

Emotion is a huge driver of social sharing. People share when they feel joy but also when they feel afraid and uncertain. In an analysis of the IPA dataBANK of 1,400 case studies of successful advertising campaigns, the cases with purely emotional content performed about twice as well (31 percent versus 16 percent) as those with only rational content.[5]

Individuals get the most benefit from participating in the social web for intangible, emotional, psychological reasons. The addictive nature of this place is born from a primal need for connection, storytelling, commiseration, and ego ... not personal financial gain.

In his book *Fizz,* word-of-mouth marketing expert Ted Wright concludes that those who ignite content are *intrinsically* motivated. "Influencers share stories because they want to build bonds with people. For them, that is the reward, and it comes from a place deep within them. If they think what you're selling will be interesting to people they know, that is all the motivation they need. You cannot buy their interest—or their approval—with discounts or rewards."

Lee Odden, the CEO of TopRank Marketing, takes the idea a step further: "Marketers talk about all these really clever ways of creating content, more and more content ... really imaginative ways of creating a diverse array of content types with nominal resources, and nowhere in these discussions do they ever really say anything. The most important characteristic of content marketing today is not quality or quantity. It's insight. And that is the differentiator lacking almost everywhere."

Think about the implications for marketing success: If most of the value creation on the social web is driven by emotion, ego, insight, and personal fulfillment—not discounts and coupons—what does that mean for *your* marketing strategy in an information dense world? For many seasoned marketers, this is a tough question and a challenging new mindset to grasp.

Connection and wearable content

Perhaps you should start thinking about your content as if it were a favorite pair of jeans. On the surface, all jeans are very similar. They're made from denim cloth, typically blue, and have two legs and a zipper. When some people buy jeans, they might be only concerned with the economic delivery system—that is, how can I cover my bum for the least amount of money possible?

But most people don't think that way. They choose jeans that say something about them. There is some intangible, tribal, emotional connection between people and their clothing. In fact, almost every decision we make in our lives, including what to wear, what to eat, and what to drive, reinforces a message we want to deliver about who we are.

For example, Wrangler has been creating a series of commercials depicting American athletes wearing their jeans in settings that are masculine, fun, and "real." They don't talk about the price, the strength of the material, or even where you can buy the product. In this case, Wrangler is selling an image to a group of men, and perhaps women who buy for men, which reinforces idealized views of the all-American male.

Similarly, people make content choices based on what the content says about them.

If you're one of the spectacular readers who tweet or post about this book to your audience, it's probably because what I've written creates a connection that is psychologically consistent with what you believe and how you want to present yourself to others. Sharing an idea from this book makes a statement about you, just like your choice in jeans, car, or a soft drink. It says, I concur. I am aligned. I think this author is smart, and I am smart; therefore, I will share it. This book is cool, and I am cool, so I will share it.

Your content becomes part of your audience's personal narrative.

Consider an example from my personal life. I noticed that many of my "cool kid friends" on Facebook were binge-watching the television series *Breaking Bad*. I began to watch this show because I was curious and didn't want to be left out of the cool conversations.

As I became engrossed in the show, I posted my progress on my social networks as a type of social currency to demonstrate that I too am part of this TV series cult. It wasn't a conscious act, but the content I consumed and shared subtly became part of my identity. For me, Breaking Bad became wearable content. It was a piece of my identity like my jeans or favorite sweater.

Consuming and sharing content normally creates an emotional benefit, not a financial one. Can you see why this presents a colossal obstacle, as companies try to use content to create *financial benefits* for themselves instead of *emotional benefits* for their readers? Doesn't this completely overturn the traditional business view of what content should accomplish?

A generation of "me-formers"

Those emotion-focused conversations are already out there by the millions. About 50 percent of what people talk about on social media is "me" focused.[6] It's more than just vanity. Studies show we're literally hard-wired to talk about ourselves. Harvard neuroscientists Jason Mitchell and Diana Tamir[7] discovered that disclosing information about ourselves is intrinsically rewarding. They found that sharing personal opinions activates the same brain circuits that respond to rewards like food and money. In another study by these researchers, they demonstrated that the power to share about ourselves is so important people are actually willing to pay money to do it.

Before the social media era, research into everyday conversation revealed that a third of it was devoted to oneself, but today that topic has become an obsession. Rutgers University researchers classify 80 percent of Twitter users as "me-formers" who tweet mainly about themselves.[8]

How can your company join that conversation? How do you ride this wave of euphoric "me-talk" and get your content, products, and brands into that powerful dialogue?

One of the best books on this topic (and one of the best recent business books, period) is *Contagious* by Dr. Jonah Berger. This important book is based on a research paper[9] Berger wrote with Katherine Milkman of The University of Pennsylvania.

In *Contagious*, Berger establishes three key strategies to help create social currency—the wearable content—that gives people a way to make themselves look good while promoting you and your ideas along the way.

1. Identify your inner remarkability.

Did you know that vending machines kill four times as many people each year than sharks? Or that the average human has more than five pounds of bacteria in their body? Or that seahorses are monogamous life mates? You probably didn't, but people like to share information like this because it's remarkable. And talking about remarkable things makes people feel remarkable. Berger explains: "Some people like to be the life of the party, but no one wants to be the death of it. We all want to be liked. The desire for social approval is a fundamental human motivation. If we tell someone a cool fact it makes us seem more engaging. If we tell someone about a secret bar hidden inside a hot dog restaurant, it makes us seem cool.

Sharing extraordinary, novel, or entertaining stories makes people seem more extraordinary, novel, and entertaining."

Berger and a fellow researcher also tested this theory among 6,500 products and brands—from huge global banks to local bagel shops. Not surprisingly, he found a hierarchy of "conversationability" among different companies. More remarkable products like Facebook and Hollywood movies were talked about twice as much less remarkable brands like banks and over-the-counter medicine.

In a study of organic Facebook reach conducted by AgoraPulse,[10] the company found that across 8,000 companies, there was definitely a pecking order of conversationability. *Organic reach* is the content that is naturally connecting to customers without any promotion. Here is a list of the industry categories with the highest organic reach:

1. Amateur sports teams
2. Farming/agriculture
3. Fashion designer
4. Professional athletes
5. Music industry
6. Building products
7. Professional sports team
8. Photographers
9. Zoos and animal-related businesses
10. Television programs

And here are the industries with the lowest Facebook organic reach:

1. Appliances
2. Books
3. Telecommunications
4. Household supplies
5. Tools and equipment
6. Phone/tablet
7. Chef
8. Musical instruments
9. Industrials
10. Transportation and freight

There is an implicit hierarchy of conversation popularity across industries. If you are in sports, entertainment, or any of the other industries in the first list, there is an implied, fervent fascination with your content. There is something that people find naturally remarkable about you that gets rewarded with content transmission. If you're in the second list or somewhere in between, you have less of an organic opportunity for social sharing ... not necessarily because of the job you're doing with your content, but because your products just aren't naturally conversational.

There is another option. If you're in an industry with relatively low organic reach, can you *become* remarkable? It doesn't come easily or cheaply, but it is possible, as evidenced by the series of "Will It Blend?" videos produced by BlendTec blenders. A blender isn't the most remarkable product, but the brand made it so through its wacky challenge ... ripping apart the most unusual things (golf balls, iPhones) in its powerful blender.

One of my favorite examples of a company overcoming a low place on the remarkability continuum is the Chipotle restaurant chain, which sells burritos and tacos—nearly commodity products in the food business. Chipotle began producing two-minute animated mini-movies telling a story of their restaurant as an oasis of natural goodness in an otherwise bleak and dystopian world of processed food. The first episode, a clay animation video with a soundtrack of Willie Nelson singing a Coldplay song, was extraordinarily popular with Chipotle's youthful audience and garnered nearly 9 million views in a year. The next year, the company went a step further by creating a free smartphone game to go with a new video. It had 4 million views in the *first week*.

Reality check: All this was created to sell *burritos*. It wasn't easy to become a conversational brand. It wasn't cheap either. But it worked, and Chipotle's stock and market share soared. That's the nice thing about remarkability: You can apply it to almost anything.

The key to finding your remarkability is to think about what makes you surprising, interesting, or novel. In my book *Social Media Explained*, I suggest that marketing strategy needs to begin by finishing this sentence: "Only we ..." That's a tough task, but it's the essential path to discover your remarkability.

In the case of Chipotle, the "only we" was creating a story of health and sustainability, a story far bigger than mere burritos and tacos. They broke a pattern of what people expected from fast food.

Marketing strategy expert Jason Falls contends that creating conversational content means invoking a "holy smokes" reaction. "Does your content make people say 'Holy smokes' because this content is so unbelievably: incredible/sad/ awesome/beautiful/intelligent/informative or some other declarative response? If that's the case, they probably need to share that content with their friends."

2. Help people achieve something with your content.

A second point in the Berger research on social currency explains why status translates into social transmission:

"Just like many other animals, people care about hierarchy. Apes engage in status displays and dogs try to figure out who is the alpha. Humans are no different. We like feeling that we're high status, top dog, or leader of the pack. But status is inherently relational. Being the leader of the pack requires a pack, and doing better than others."

He suggests that building game mechanics into your content strategy might push people into transmission mode. Examples of content activities that bestow accomplishment include:

- Achieving a status level
- Winning an award
- Being included on a "best of" list
- Getting a high score on a quiz
- Being favorably mentioned in a video, podcast, or post

Achieving status helps generate social currency and social sharing. After all, what good is accomplishing something if you can't tell people about it?

Word of mouth also can come from the voting process itself. Deciding the winner by popular vote encourages contestants to drum up support. But in telling people to vote for them, contestants also spread awareness about the product sponsoring the contest. Instead of marketing yourself directly, you use the contest to get people who want to win to do the marketing themselves.

One of the most interesting competitions I've seen is the "Top Social Media Blog Contest" compiled by Social Media Examiner, one of the top sites on the marketing scene. The unique aspect of this blog is that it routinely highlights competitor blogs.

Michael Stelzner, the company founder, explained that the unusual contest drives web traffic, but there are other benefits: "It's good for our business to recognize bloggers who do an outstanding job with their content. I don't see any conflict in recognizing competing blogs to our own. Instead, I have the view that all ships rise when more attention is brought to those doing great work for the industry.

"In many cases, the winners of the Top Social Media Blog Contest have told us that getting on the list has been a big goal of their business, or it has literally helped propel their industry stature and authority. Of course this drives an enormous amount of interest and traffic to the site but there are other benefits. First, it helps us identify up-and-coming thought leaders who we may want to have on our podcasts or speak at our events. Second, it is a gift of sorts that establishes a lot of good will with those who are finalists and winners. Third, the winners post award badges on their sites, providing more exposure for our brand."

In this example, Social Media Examiner effectively helps people achieve status with its content, and it sends their content transmission sky high.

Another common tool for creating personal achievement through content is quizzes, which explains why they appear on so many sites that depend on advertising for their revenues. In 2014, eight of the 10 most-shared articles on the entire Internet were quizzes. Sharing positive or funny quiz results fuels our identity and ego. Others learn more about who we are, what we value, and our tastes.

MIT cultural analyst Sherry Turkle[11] says that people turn to quizzes to fulfill an irresistible need to quantify the human condition. "Basically, we're trying to get a number," she said. "And people will use a quiz to get that number. It gives people something to look at, an object to think with." She adds that people have always loved quizzes, but in the pre-social media days, we primarily took them for ourselves. "Now they're specifically for performance," she said. "Part of the point is to share it … It's the conflation of who you are and who thinks you're okay."

So when you're making quizzes for your audience, you're giving them an opportunity to learn something interesting about themselves *and* a chance to start a conversation with their friends. It's hard to say that about a lot of other forms of content.

3. Make it exclusive.

In a web world where you want the content to flow freely, how do you use exclusivity—holding content back—to your advantage?

Information is abundant, and almost any content can easily be found for free. For any person or company trying to monetize scarce or premium content on the social web, there is always somebody else out there willing to provide the same webinar, video, or eBook for nothing, destroying your idea of a scarce resource. Chris Anderson's book *Free: The Future of a*

Radical Price codifies this idea by basically saying "get used to it"—you have to find adjacencies and other revenue streams because people expect Internet-based content and services to be free.

Is there *anything* scarce on the Internet?

Yes, there is, according to digital marketing savant Christopher S. Penn of SHIFT Communications. "Scarcity is actually more powerful than ever on the social web," he said. "While content may be free, what has become extremely scarce is time, attention, and influence. These are hot commodities, rare commodities. As an example, I have tens of thousands of followers on Twitter. I can't tell you the number of direct messages and tweets, Facebook messages, and emails I receive every day asking, 'Hey, can you promote my whatever' because they know that it means something. Moving content creates true value. So in that regard, scarcity is a weapon that is in play like never before."

On the other side of the coin, providing exclusive or limited access to content can create the perception of scarcity that can make the content move.

Scarcity and exclusivity boost word of mouth by making people feel like insiders. If people get something rare, it makes them feel special, unique, and high status. And because of that, they'll not only like a product or service more, but tell others about it more. Why? Because telling others makes them look good. Having insider knowledge is social currency. When people who waited hours in line finally get that new tech gadget, one of the first things they do is show others. Look at me and what I was able to get!

As the publisher of a popular blog, I am deluged with requests to try new products and services. I ignore these pitches because I know the same email is being sent to a thousand other people. Why would I create content on a subject that could appear in hundreds of other blogs the next day? I want something exclusive. I want to be an insider.

But there is one type of content that makes me stop, pay attention, and share what's being offered—exclusive insight. Here are three examples of companies who used "first access" as an effective way to transmit their information:

- When a well-known digital analytics company was acquired by a large international firm, their PR team set up an exclusive opportunity for me to interview the company's founder right after the announcement. I wrote a lengthy post about the company and its prospects in the new organization ... I moved their content!

- Another company offered me an in-person meeting with a team developing their new cognitive computing platform. I have used exclusive insights from this discussion in blog posts, speeches, and college classes.

- Joe Pulizzi of the Content Marketing Institute does a wonderful job creating research reports that are both useful and insightful. He releases the research early to a select group of bloggers so they can prepare their content before the general release of the information. Even though the research is shared with a relatively large mailing list, I can usually zero in on some finding to focus on for a unique blog post.

There is a third aspect to this scarcity/exclusivity factor that will become more important to content transmission in coming years—context, or *microsegmentation*.

Marketers can now identify subsections of consumers who fall within their targeted audience through a combination of advanced algorithms, artificial intelligence, and data mining. You can use this microsegmentation to personalize and focus communication and marketing campaigns, making them more relevant to consumers at their point of need.

Individuals have unique reasons for identifying and interacting with your brand—their feelings about your products, promotions, and services vary with their momentary interests and motivations. Microsegmentation attempts to recognize the individual needs and drill down to the motivating factors that enable you to craft appealing and relevant messages.

Krista LaRiviere, the Cofounder and CEO of gShift, a Toronto-based web presence analytics company, leads a team that has developed a process to help companies develop "smart" micro-segmented content:

Step 1: Deconstruct the segment conversations

- Analyze the over-arching sentiment of this segment. What do they love, hate, embrace, reject?
- Familiarize yourself with the iconic brands, products, and services that are associated with this group.
- Discover conversational triggers that relate to the benefits of your brand: problems, solutions, functions, benefits

Step 2: Examine and understand the segment's conversational language

- Can your content address customer needs in their nuanced language?
- By researching social media platforms and online forums, can you determine the very specific likes, dislikes, and pain points this segment is discussing?
- What are the key places, conversations, and keywords that connect your company with that micro-segment?

Step 3: Craft your focused micro-segment content

- Build on themes, concerns, and trends highlighted from the research
- Use the native language and idioms of that segment
- Identify like-minded employees, or influencers, who can naturally engage with that micro-segment

By creating messages in context, content can be delivered to your consumer because of where she is, who she is, relevant announcements she cares about, and breaking news events. Having that type of useful information builds social currency and is a powerful motivator to share.

We're approaching an era when the information we need most will be coming to us—we won't have to search for it. It will be an Internet, instead of an Internet. Watch how Amazon anticipates your needs. That's how the Internet will be conforming to you soon.

A fourth way to use exclusivity to your advantage is to create communities help consumers connect with each other—not just with your brand. *The New York Times* research defined high-potential sharers by six categories of people who tend to band together on the web:

- **Altruists:** Altruistic sharers are people who want to be seen as helpful and reliable. They're thoughtful and well-connected. Their primary method for sharing content is through email.

- **Careerists:** Careerists want to be seen as valuable and upwardly-mobile. They want to share content that makes them seem intelligent and well-connected. A primary platform for them is LinkedIn.

- **Hipsters:** Hipsters regard content sharing as an integral part of who they are. They're the least likely group to use email and lean toward Twitter and emerging social media platforms. This is a youthful group who wants to be seen as creative and cutting edge.

- **Boomerangs:** Boomerangs are highly validated by the reactions they get from their posts. They want to be provocative and earn attention through the reactions of others. They're heavy users of both Twitter and Facebook.

- **Connectors:** Connectors are social butterflies who love to bring people and ideas together. They're planners who are typically relaxed, creative, and thoughtful. They most often share content through email and Facebook.

- **Selectives:** As the name implies, Selectives don't share with vast social audiences. They will share a piece of content with select individuals who they think would benefit from it, usually via email. They're resourceful, careful, and informed and want to be seen as useful and thoughtful.

How can you create content that will appeal to these personas? Are there standard processes you can build into your content to make it more likely to ignite? That's what the next chapter is all about!

CHAPTER FOUR

22 Practical Ways to Achieve Content Ignition

"Average brands advertise. Great brands share."
– Ted Wright

I n this chapter, we'll continue exploring the idea of embedding shareability into your content and focus on 22 quick-hit actions you can use right away.

Social recommendations from friends and family are the most trusted source of information for consumers according to eConsultancy.[1] When your customers share positive opinions and experiences on social media, they increase your credibility among potential customers in a way you, as a business, can never accomplish alone. So you need to do whatever you can to make it easy for those transmissions to flow.

The basic idea behind this chapter is removing every possible obstacle in your control so there is simply no excuse not to share your content! You're sure to find at least a few ideas you can put to work for your business right away.

Here we go.

1. Push the right buttons.

Sadly, I must begin this list with what should be the most obvious recommendation ... but perhaps the most useful: Add social sharing buttons to your content site.

Does that seem like odd advice? When I help businesses with their social media strategy, *half* of them don't have social sharing buttons on their websites—even very large companies! In this case, the organizations are almost challenging their readers to share the content by denying them the convenience of a simple share button! A recent study[2] showed that content with sharing buttons is 700 percent more likely to spread than content without those buttons.

Make sure your social button widget doesn't require multiple clicks to complete the share, or use a bare link as a snippet in a tweet. I've seen some Twitter buttons that just tweet the link without the title or the site/author's name, which is a missed opportunity for free PR.

As I explain in Chapter 3, some personality types prefer email for social transmission, so add one of those buttons, too.

2. Tear down those walls!

Many companies create a firewall that forces you to opt-in for content by signing in with an email address or trading even more personal information.

I can understand the logic of this approach. If I'm providing value to you (through my content), you need to provide value to me (through an email address so I can send you offers and updates). The problem is, this strategy turns many people away. The number varies widely by industry, but research states that between 25 percent and 90 percent of your customers turn away if they need to register first to obtain what they're looking for. In one user interface experiment, a large company found that removing the need to register for content increased sales by $300 million.[3]

If you're in the business of igniting your content, why would you throw water on the flame by requiring people to divulge personal information first? That issue is the tip of a larger iceberg question: If I give away my content and best ideas with nothing in return, am I just giving away my business? Let's address this issue.

On the right side of my blog, there's a prompt called "Categories" where you can peruse hundreds of blog posts by topic. For example, under the category of "blogging best practices," you can view more than 180 posts. I also have a free blogging eBook available on my site and have done numerous podcasts and webinars on blogging ... all of them completely free.

In a couple of hours, you can probably learn every idea and concept I've ever had about blogging by mining these free resources. And yet, somebody calls me every week willing to pay for blog coaching. I do social media workshops on content creation with many large companies. I'm paid to give speeches on the topic all the time. And lots of folks are still buying my comprehensive book *Born to Blog*.

This doesn't make sense, does it? How can I make money dispensing blogging advice when I'm giving away every blogging tip and secret I ever had?

Business relationships are built on trust. They always have been. But for centuries you were limited by time and geography. You could only create trust with those who actually knew you—and probably within a pretty small area. The social web is an incredible gift to businesses everywhere. For the first time in history, you can create relationships and build trust with people far and wide ... through your voice, your views, and your expertise. But the only way to do that is by giving them enough free content to know you and trust you.

When I started my consulting business, I took all the business I could get on a regional level. Slowly my business evolved and grew, completely on the back of my blog content. And now I have connections all over the world through social media. In fact, I've never spent one dime on any form of advertising for my consulting business. In other words, my business has grown *only* because I give everything away!

Unlock your content. Unleash it. Tear down those walls. And watch your business grow!

3. Be entertaining, funny, and inspiring.

There's a very good reason people share pictures of puppies.

Psychoanalyst Donald Winnicott discovered that our first emotional action in life is to respond to our mother's smile with a smile of our own. A desire for joy and happiness is hardwired into all of us. Joy can also be a driver of action. Winnicott's discovery of a baby's "social smile" also tells us that joy increases when it is shared.

No wonder, then, that happiness is an important driver for social media sharing. Think about the content you like to spread to your friends or online tribe. A lot of it is joyful, funny, or entertaining, right? Well, turns out there are a lot of people like you out there! Research into the most-shared articles on the web[4] uncovers three primary emotions in the content:

- Awe (25%)
- Laughter (17%)
- Amusement/entertainment (15%)

Pew Research[5] reports that 35 percent of men and 43 percent of women are on Facebook primarily to see entertaining or funny posts.

This idea also shows up in the Berger/Milkman research.[6] They found that content with a positive sentiment tends to go viral more than negative content. It's more complex than that of course—people share content that expresses a wide range of emotions—but in general, staying positive should help you trend toward better shareability.

Research by the company AgoraPulse[7] found that the most-shared posts on Facebook also had some element of inspiration in them, indicated by keywords like:

- **Give:** Offers, discounts, deals, or contests that can benefit a wide audience.
- **Advice:** Tips, especially about problems that everyone encounters. Examples are how to lose weight or how to choose a college.

- **Warning:** Posts about dangers that could affect anyone in your audience.
- **Inspire:** Inspirational quotes. Love them or hate them, they work.
- **Unite:** Posts that highlight a danger, an evil, an enemy, a cause, or a personal or community need.

And while we're at it, the research also showed content behaviors that shut down social sharing (don't do these!):

- Only talking about yourself
- Being too edgy or offensive
- Being too obscure or niche
- Publishing content nobody can understand
- Asking for Likes

4. Go long.

Every marketing trend seems to point to a need for short content. Six-second Vine videos. High-level infographics. Tweets that top out at 140 characters. Shorter content enables social sharing in a busy world, right? Not necessarily.

According to an analysis[8] of 100 million web-based articles, long-form content actually gets shared more than short-form content. In fact, the longer the content, the more shares it may get, with pieces of 3,000–10,000 words getting the highest average shares of any category. Research by the *New York Times* confirms this trend; more than 90 percent of their most-emailed articles are more than 3,000 words long.

Not surprisingly, short-form content abounds—there are 16 times more articles with less than 1,000 words than there are with 2,000+ words. Here's your opportunity to fill the gap.

When writing long-form content, remember to make it easy to scan—no one likes an intimidating wall of text. Using a list structure is a simple way to do that. Write short, easy-to-read paragraphs, and use subheadings and bullet points to break up the text. Bonus tip: Using a keyword in a subheading normally provides some SEO value.

5. Aim for conversation, not controversy.
Without question, controversy ignites content. A few consultants even recommend that you consistently manufacture controversial content as a legitimate ignition strategy. Controversial content can fascinate people the same way that a good feud on reality television drives up ratings. But I don't think this is a sustainable strategy.

First, let me distinguish content that is conversational or thought-provoking from content that is controversial. A definition of *controversial* is "a state of prolonged, contentious public dispute or debate." The keywords here for me are "prolonged," "contentious, and "public."

Sometimes controversy is unavoidable. But is this a tactic you should mindfully pursue as a long-term content strategy? Can you think of any respected, successful company that pursues a prolonged dispute as a marketing strategy? Of course not. Companies are built to *avoid* controversy. Most brands are not built on a negative emotion. Study after study shows that positive, uplifting content gets more views and clicks over time.

Another argument against controversy as a social transmission strategy is that it may attract the wrong audience. Controversial blog posts are like a schoolyard fight. The fascination value may drive a short-term spike in traffic, but will it make somebody want to befriend you? Become a customer? Or, will they just stay on the sidelines and walk away when the fight is over?

Controversy can be used most effectively when it is associated with a positive cause. The CVS pharmacy chain raised a ruckus when it banned cigarette sales from its stores as part of its focus on wellness. Clothing retailer Patagonia defied conventional business logic by recommending that its customers purchase less clothing, buy better quality items, and reuse, repair, resell, and recycle to be environmentally friendly.

6. Remember that the most important part of your content is not your content.

Do you want to increase the shareability of your content by 400 percent in one easy step? Lean in close now as I share this secret: Stop writing sucky headlines.

In today's world, you *must* craft a descriptive, emotive, accurate, catchy, and "tweet-able" headline. This is so fundamental yet it remains a challenge for many content creators. The headline is more important than the video or body of the text. Why? Because we live in a world of scanners, and if you can't grab somebody by the throat in a nanosecond, you've lost them. They will never see the rest of the post.

So here's the official Content Code Ever-So-Useful List of Best Blog Post Headline Practices:

- Make it tweetable (i.e. short). Headlines with eight words or less are shared 21 percent more than average.[9]
- Make it descriptive and accurate. Never mislead readers.

- Make it creative enough to stand out in a crowded list of content choices.
- Reference a numbered list to increase social transmission by 50 percent (like: "Six Extraordinary Lessons from The Content Code").
- Make sure the headline offers something helpful.
- Include one keyword or phrase to help a search engine determine the theme of the article and aid your SEO.
- Don't let your headline be an afterthought. The headline is the most critical part of the post. Work it.

Warm words help, too. In a study of blog posts that had received more than 1,000 social shares over a year, headlines that featured a "human" word like "food," "home," and "lifestyle" accounted for 85 percent of the world's most viral content. Words like "business," "tech," and "news" made up just 14 percent of this traffic.[10] A useful tool to use when creating headlines is the free Headline Analyzer from the Advanced Marketing Institute (http://bit.ly/headlineanalyze). It works on the theory that increasing the emotional marketing value (EMV) of your headline drives more social sharing. In my independent research, I've found that social sharing drops off if the headline is too emotional. The ideal score seems to center between 30 and 50 points.

7. Be visual.
Read a piece of information, and three days later you'll remember 10 percent of it. Add a picture and you'll remember 65 percent.[11] Reading is inefficient for humans. Your brain sees

words as lots of tiny pictures, and then you have to identify features in the letters to read them. That takes time.

According to a BuzzSumo analysis, adding a photo or illustration doubles the probability that your content will get shared. Another study verifies that when using Facebook as your content distribution channel, sharing of the content is doubled, on average, if you include a photo. Naturally, brands are figuring this out—74 percent of all Facebook brand posts now contain a photo.[12]

When formatting a photo for a blog post, most blogging platforms give you the chance to assign a meta tag or "alternative text" to the photos. Attaching the keyword or theme from the article to the photo doesn't take much time and can provide a small SEO boost.

8. Ignite with lists and infographics.

The BuzzSumo research of 100 million posts also showed that you double your chances that people will share your content if it includes a list or an infographic. It makes sense. Both list posts and infographics add an element of intrigue and fun while still promising quick answers. Because of their skimmable format, they satisfy our curiosity quickly in an information-dense environment.

Bonus tip: A list article with the number 10 in the headline is the best number for social transmission, scoring *four times* the social shares as the next nearest number in the study. After the number 10, list headlines with an odd-number get shared 20 percent more than even-numbered posts.[13]

9. Boost social sharing with suggested stories.

In this book I shy away from recommending specific technologies because they'll become obsolete at some point and I don't want to date the book unnecessarily. But there is one little plug-in that delivers so much punch that it deserves a shout-out: LinkedWithin.

It takes a lot of work to get somebody to visit your site, so once you get them there, do what you can to keep them there. A great way to do that is to use a free widget like LinkedWithin to suggest similar content for your readers. At the bottom of each post it lists relevant articles from your blog for your readers to enjoy. It has four powerful benefits:

- It effectively resurrects relevant older content, giving you more bang for your content investment.
- It can increase page views. I haven't been able to find any universal data on this benefit, but for me, LinkedWithin increases page views on my site by 8 percent. That's HUGE!
- By taking your readers more deeply into relevant content, it increases the chances of connection, subscription, or perhaps even clicks into commercial parts of your site.
- It increases social sharing. It's not unusual to see new readers to my blog tweet three, four, or more stories in a matter of a few minutes as they go from post to post via LinkedWithin.

Bonus tip: LinkedWithin uses an image from your old posts as a visual prompt to keep customers clicking ... another great reason to always include a photo or graphic with your content.

10. Revive content.

One of the most depressing aspects of content creation is its short shelf life. I actually had one person tweet to me "Great post—even though it's older content." The post was only two weeks old!

Research demonstrates that social sharing on a post is usually over by the fourth day. In fact, after three days, the number of social shares drops by at least 96 percent across every major social network. But the demise of your content is not inevitable.

Here's an example of content that breaks the "death cycle." A few months ago I noticed something startling in my statistics. Over the life of my Twitter account, a total of 100,000 people had unfollowed me! As I dug into it, I discovered there was a sub-culture of people who do mass Twitter following and then mass unfollowing. Well, butter my buns and call me a biscuit. All that unfollowing had nothing to do with me after all! It was a residual effect of people trying to "game" Twitter!

I thought this would make a provocative blog post[14] and I had some fun with the headline: "Why 100,000 People Unfollowed Me on Twitter." But it was also a very helpful post that answered a lot of questions people had about this strange behavior.

Here are the total social sharing statistics (Twitter, Facebook, LinkedIn and Google+) for the post:

Month of Publication	Total Number of Shares
April 2013	378
September 2013	654
December 2013	1,012
March 2014	1,144
September 2014	1,858
January 2015	2,020

How is this possible? If most blog posts die after four days, how did this content keep chugging and chugging, finding new fans for years?

There's a lot of sharing potential stored in content that is always relevant and useful. This *evergreen content* answers your customers' most common questions and rarely goes out-of-date. For example, a "Mommy Jogger" blog would feature evergreen content that describes the correct use of jogging strollers. This post would be useful and relevant to customers for years ... and could also be re-posted as new people look for the content.

And that is exactly what I did. I could see that my "Unfollow" post was popular, evergreen content that people enjoyed, so I tweeted the link out to my audience about once a month. And each time I did, it received more comments and social shares. *A lot* more!

This is an obvious strategy many businesses ignore because they feel strange about posting "old" content. But you need to view evergreen content as an investment in an asset for your business. If you bought a new tractor for your farm or a new truck for your plumbing business, you wouldn't just let it sit around not being used. An investment in content is no different. Use it!

There aren't any hard and fast rules about sharing your most popular evergreen content but every other month seems about right. If you have enough of these pieces in your arsenal, you can build an evergreen content promotion schedule.

Bonus tip: There are WordPress plugins available to help you schedule and re-post your most popular content for months into the future. Igniting content with no work? I like it!

11. Determine the best posting time.

Don't fall for blog posts with lists of the "best times to post." The fact is that the ultimate time to post is highly sensitive to a number of factors, and you need to do the work to figure out the best posting schedule specific to your business and customer base.

While a general search on the topic might lead you to believe that the best day to publish on LinkedIn is Wednesday or the best day to promote on Facebook is Monday, the truth is that sharing peaks on different days in every vertical. Here are just a few examples of sharing trends by industry:[15]

- Publications in the automotive vertical earn the most shares on Wednesday.
- General business publications see the most shares on Tuesday.
- Health industry articles show peak engagement on Tuesdays and Fridays.
- Food-related posts get shared the most on Mondays.
- The weekends are a low point for sharing in every vertical, rarely earning more than 9 percent of shares.

And of course you can throw all of these guidelines out the door if you're trying to post at times and in spaces unoccupied by competitors. I noticed that one of my blogging friends posted every Sunday. This seemed counter-intuitive since blog posts usually get the *least* amount of traction on weekends. His logic was simple: "All the established bloggers post on Monday, so to stand out, I'm posting on a day that's less crowded." A very sensible approach. He's finding an unsaturated niche based on the day of the week!

12. Re-purpose content.

Evergreen content is a versatile workhorse and can be re-purposed to create new information forms for your customers. A series of evergreen posts can be compiled, edited, and offered as an in-depth special report. You can also turn the evergreen posts into speeches, webinars, videos, and email courses—just to name a few ideas.

You can transform a piece of research or a dataset into an infographic, and an infographic into a video, and a video into a podcast, and a podcast transcript into a blog post, and a blog post into a press release. Every piece of content can be altered for a different medium with minimal additional investment. This means more content, gaining exposure with new audiences, in less time.

One technique that has had blockbuster results for me is turning my best "old" content into colorful presentations on SlideShare. My original blog post "Six questions that lead you to a social media strategy" had a total of about 7,000 page views. After I posted it on SlideShare, the same content has been seen more than 100,000 times! SlideShare is free to use, owned by LinkedIn, highly indexed by Google, and a deep educational resource for many people. At the end of that particular presentation, I had a call to action to learn more by buying my book *Social Media Explained*. I could easily track this link to see how many clicks I received.

Best of all, by re-purposing the content on a new channel, I was reaching an entirely new audience who had never seen the first post. I also ignited a new round of social sharing on the same investment with very little development cost.

Here are a few more ways to re-purpose and re-ignite your content with little or no incremental expense:

- Narrate existing slide presentations and turn them into YouTube videos.
- Take the audio from videos and use it in podcasts.
- Assemble blog posts into themes to create helpful eBooks and customer guides.
- Use blog content as a starter for book chapters.
- Turn list posts into infographics.
- Post infographics on SlideShare and Pinterest.

13. Focus on feedback and reviews.[16]

Another important form of social transmission is feedback and reviews. Reviews offer powerful "social proof" that can make or break a business. This concept is covered extensively in Chapter 9 but in short, social proof is an accumulation of the clues in our environment we use to make decisions when we don't know the truth. Reviews are a good example of this idea. If we have never visited a business before, we may turn to this crowd-sourced content to decide whether to buy something or not.

For many businesses, online reviews are a high-stakes component of consumer decision-making. Car shoppers, for example, are increasingly relying on Yelp and other ratings sites. Nielsen reports[17] that 84 percent of people say that online reviews influence their buying decision. These reviewers can even gain celebrity status as their opinions reverberate throughout Twitter, Facebook, and beyond.

The key with this tactic is to have a rock-solid internal process for capturing and maintaining a steady stream of customers willing to write reviews. Understandably, many of your frontline sales personnel may feel awkward about asking for a review, but you can put it in a way that makes the customer comfortable: "Our business is based on referrals. Would you take a moment to visit Yelp and refer us to your friends and family?" This is a great start to your internal process, but it's only the beginning.

Here are several ways to improve social transmission through Yelp and other review sites:

- **Designate someone to take ownership of your implementation plan.** This person is in charge of your online reputation and is responsible for getting grassroots participation from your staff, as well as monitoring and responding to the community.
- **Use signage and memos.** Create awareness with your customers and your staff. Display "Love Us on Yelp!" signs throughout the store—entryways, sales offices, customer waiting area, customer service, and check-out. Give customers a card to take with them that reminds them you're on Yelp. Put memos on

paychecks, repair orders, and invoices to create awareness.

- **Reach out to your raving fans.** Every salesperson has them, especially those who have been with you a long time. Ask fans to share an honest review—don't push for positive reviews, per se. Many brands fail to feature testimonials and brand evangelists on their websites and social media profiles. People love attention and special treatment—the customers you feature will likely become even stronger supporters of your brand. Plus, showcasing objective opinions on your website may increase your credibility among potential customers.

- **Consider hosting a customer of the week program on your blog and on social media.** Feature a story and testimonial from one of your satisfied customers.

- **Hold a monthly contest with the staff.** Nothing motivates like a cash prize! For example, if the store gets 20 reviews by the end of the month, you'll draw a name and that person wins the cash.

- **Recognize staff members who get 5-star reviews.** A gift or a nice mention during the weekly sales meeting goes a long way. When the other employees see it, they'll be eager to be recognized, too.

14. Be practical.

In Chapter 1, I recounted the story of the Mirabeau Miracle. The winery's proprietor, Stephen Cronk, made YouTube history with a 90-second video showing how to open a wine bottle with his shoe.

This was not epic content. It wasn't even original. The trick had been done multiple times before on YouTube. The Mirabeau case study doesn't seem to follow any rules about emotion or storytelling. But it's an amazing, well-executed little demonstration, and it was a practical, useful tip.

In the book *Contagious*, Jonah Berger explains, "Today, direct opportunities to help others are few and far between. Modern suburban life has distanced us from our friends and neighbors. We live at the end of a long driveway or high up in an apartment building, often barely getting to know the person next door.

"But sharing something useful with others is a quick and easy way to help people out, even if we're not in the same place. Parents can send their kids useful advice even if they are hundreds of miles away. Passing along useful things strengthen social bonds. Our friends see we know and care about them, we feel good for being helpful, and the sharing cements our friendship."

People love to help their friends save money, so building extraordinary value or a deal into your content is a way to help it move. Not surprisingly, the bigger the perceived deal or the more exclusive it appears, the more the content moves.

Curation is another good way to provide practical content. Curating or summarizing valuable content by industry, career discipline, or interest saves people time because you've done the work to filter content for them. In the pharmaceutical industry, summaries of new surgical or medical breakthroughs are a good way to bond with doctors and provide truly useful information. Several wealth management companies curate global financial information to make the world of investing less complicated. You can find opportunities to curate along any interest you can imagine.

15. Learn to use hashtags effectively.

Hashtags are arguably the most important innovation in the history of social media. The humble hashtag has become the index card system of the web. It's social media's most important way to organize information, and it's critical to discovering trends, content, and ideas. Hashtags have crept into popular culture, and brands now feature them on advertisements, TV shows, billboards, menus, and even on the big screen at sporting events.

Following a hashtag also organizes people. The people following a hashtag might be starting a company, leading a discussion that leads to innovation, or planning the overthrow of a government. Hashtags are the cornerstone elements for communicating everything from disaster relief to memes. They can also be an important element in the Content Code equation. Research indicates that the presence of a hashtag could increase social transmission by as much as 70 percent on some topics.

Here are some examples of hashtag campaigns that ignited ideas and messages:[18]

- **Charmin:** In 2013, toilet paper brand Charmin launched the Twitter hashtag #tweetfromtheseat to take advantage of the staggering number of people who use social media in the bathroom (40 percent of young adults—and those are just the ones who admit it!). Keys to success included the use of actionable language (the hashtag starts with a verb telling followers to *do* something); it was fun and playful; and it was tied to a larger Super Bowl promotion.

- **Make-A-Wish Foundation:** A few years ago, the world fell in love with 5-year-old cancer fighter Miles (aka "BatKid") when he became a superhero for a day. San Francisco became Gotham City thanks to the Greater Bay Area Make-A-Wish Foundation and the help of 16,000 actors and volunteers. Dressed in full Batman costume, BatKid saved the city from the forces of evil while hundreds of thousands of people followed along on social media with the hashtag #SFBatKid. The story blew up, generating an estimated 1.7 billion social impressions across 117 countries. Celebrities like Christian Bale, Ben Affleck, and Britney Spears used the #SFBatKid hashtag. Even President Barack Obama gave Miles a six-second shoutout on Vine. Make-A-Wish saw a huge boost in site traffic—as many as 1,400 hits per second during the peak of the campaign. The hashtag worked because it promoted an emotional story, the event was meticulously planned, and it involved thousands of volunteers who helped ignite the content.

- **DiGiorno Pizza:** No, a drunk intern didn't take over the @DiGiornoPizza Twitter handle during American football games. In fact, DiGiorno Pizza's unconventional #DiGiorNOYOUDIDNT campaign was carefully strategized. The brand came up with the hashtag idea in hopes of expanding DiGiorno Pizza's social media reach to new audiences—specifically, the NFL smack-talkers of the Twitterverse. Their staff live-tweeted during NFL games and engaged with football fans in real-time. The campaign worked because it was real-time, humorous, and associated with a popular sporting event.

16. Make it look good.

How your site looks is an important indicator of whether your content is share-worthy. When you head out for a night of fine dining, you don't expect an expensive steak to arrive in a Styrofoam container with a packet of ketchup. And you expect premium content to look like premium content, too.

Everything communicates, and if you don't have the proper container for your content, you might be killing your transmission effort before it starts. Your site is your front door to the world and the first impression that might determine whether somebody leaves right away or stays long enough to find out what you're up to.

Remember that social sharing is often an extension of self-identity. If your site is classy, people will feel classy about promoting it. If your site looks trashy ... well ... it might be time for a re-fresh!

On a related note, have you checked your Google Analytics recently to see how many customers are accessing your site via a mobile device? You may be surprised! Make sure your site is optimized to serve your customers in a mobile environment. Content consumers make quick decisions about sharing, and if it's difficult to accomplish or your sharing buttons aren't obvious in a mobile environment, you'll lose those precious opportunities.

17. Concentrate on brand new research and ideas.

Remember that many of your readers share content because of the intrinsic value of helping others. Focusing your content on new insights from research, quotes from experts, and exciting new ideas will appeal to this psychological aspect of sharing.

This is also a source of rich content creation ideas. When you see a particularly compelling piece of research, quote it, provide proper links and attribution, and then give it your own spin:

- What did you learn from this new research?
- What new ideas did this enable?
- Was the research done correctly, or is there a problem with the methodology you need to highlight?
- How can the research be practically applied to problems in your industry?
- What surprised you? What doesn't make sense? How does the research provide a new world view?

All of these personal spins on data can make compelling original content highly valued by your most passionate audience members.

18. Encourage comments.

People who care enough to leave comments on the content you publish are also highly likely to share it with their networks. If they spend the time to leave an opinion on your work, they want the world to know it, too! To the extent that you can encourage comments, you're encouraging social sharing.

Here are some easy ways to encourage people to comment:

- End your post with a question. People hate an open-ended post and are more likely to close the loop by answering your question in a comment.
- Ask specifically for comments. In Chapter 7, I cover the importance of comments and social proof, but prime the pump by asking a few friends and work colleagues to leave a comment. Comments spur comments. People feel better about leaving their views when they see they're not standing all alone in the comment section.
- Mention influencers with large audiences in your post and link to their content. Most of the time they will be "pinged" when someone links to their content, but don't be afraid to let them know the link exists. They'll probably share your post.
- Notify potential commenters. Send an email to people in your industry who would be interested in your post. You need to use this method judiciously—you can't keep going to the well until it's dry! If they trust you and the request, you'll almost certainly earn a comment and a share from these connections.

19. Tap into FOMO

Many people are obsessed with being constantly connected to the web due to a Fear of Missing Out (or FOMO). Tapping into this fear can also get people to click and share.

Here's an example of FOMO in action:[19] Marc and Angel Chernoff have an incredible blog at www.marcandangel.com. They publish inspiring content that regularly spreads across social media, garnering thousands if not hundreds of thousands of social shares. One of the most fascinating pieces they've written is a post called "30 Things to Stop Doing to Yourself" that received more than 500,000 Likes, 20,000 tweets, and several thousand shares on other social networks.

They wrote a similar post, "30 Things to Start Doing for Yourself," but the more negative one, "30 Things to Stop Doing to Yourself," performed much better. They said using negative words like "stop," "avoid," and "don't" always led to better performance. They reasoned that everyone wants to find out if they're missing out on something they should stop doing.

20. Help readers spread ideas to help others.

Here's an insight from my favorite newspaper, *The New York Times*:[20] In an attempt to understand what's buzzworthy, neuroscientists scanned the brains of people while they were hearing about new ideas. Then, as these people told others about what they had heard, the scientists observed which ideas spread and which didn't.

You might predict that people would pass along the most memorable ideas—the ones that light up the brain regions associated with memories. But that's not what happened. The best predictors of buzz were in the brain regions associated with social cognition—thoughts about other people. If those regions lit up when something was heard, people were more likely to talk about the idea enthusiastically, and the idea would keep spreading.

"You'd expect people to be most enthusiastic spreading ideas that they themselves are excited about," said researcher Dr. Emily Falk of the University of Michigan. "But our research suggests that's not the whole story. Thinking about what appeals to others may be even more important."

Abigail Posner, head of strategic planning for Google, described this urge as an energy exchange:[21] "When we see or create an image that enlivens us, we send it to others to give them a bit of energy and effervescence. Every gift holds the spirit of the gifter. Also, every image reminds us and others that we're alive, happy, and full of energy (even if we may not always feel that way). And when we Like or comment on a picture or video sent to us, we're sending a gift of sorts back to the sender. We're affirming them. But, most profoundly, this 'gift' of sharing contributes to an energy exchange that amplifies our own pleasure—and is something we're hardwired to do."

21. Include "click to tweet" boxes in your blog post.

This is a fun and easy way to increase the number of tweets you get on any article. There are several free services that allow you to embed tweetable quotes right into your blog post. Pull out the best quotes from your post, and paste them to a "click to tweet" box you can access for free on the Internet. An attractive box appears in the context of your post, encouraging readers to easily click and tweet a meaningful quote.

22. Add your personality.

In the next two chapters, we'll be exploring two intertwined BADASS factors—building an Alpha Audience and creating the Heroic Brand. Both elements require an extraordinary emotional connection to the author, brand, or company. And that is delivered through content that connects.

To stand out on the web today, you must be original. And to be original, you need to inject your personality into the content. Let's conduct a quick test. Look at the headline examples below and choose which one you're more likely to click and share:

- "Five common mistakes on Twitter" or "My biggest Twitter catastrophe"
- "Three great recipes for corn" or "How corn saved my rehearsal dinner"
- "Testing three new servers" or "How I fell hopelessly in love with cloud computing"

If you're like most people, you probably picked the second option in these examples. Even though these posts would be appropriate for a corporate blog, the headline hints at something personal, unique, and revealing. The first headlines could have been written by anyone. But the second headlines could only be written from the perspective of a real person. Create content for humans. *Create content that only you can create.*

Well, that should give you enough to work on for a few weeks. But we're just getting started! Your work to build share-ability into your content will always be sub-optimized if you don't also find and nurture an audience who is primed and ready for ignition. Let's discover a BADASS strategy to create an Alpha Audience most likely to share your content.

CHAPTER FIVE

Building an Alpha Audience

"Today, artists get record deals because they have fans – not the other way around." – Taylor Swift

Content is merely the match lighting the fuse of an ignition plan. You have to find the people to actually do it! You need to amass an *Alpha Audience*—an elite and engaged tribe at the top of the social sharing food chain, the bedrock of your business. Google research shows that these most loyal members of your audience are more than 250 percent more likely to transmit your content!

To set the stage for our important work together on this subject, I'd like to provide a short case study illustrating one of the biggest problems companies face when it comes to activating their digital audience of friends and followers.

The dysfunctional social media audience

A few years ago, I decided to try something I had never done before (or since). I asked my social media audience to donate money to support a favorite charity.

I had been working for a group that mentors inner city children, and the world financial crisis had taken a bite out of their budget at a critical time. Asking for money on the Internet is a notoriously difficult proposition. I document this extensively in my book *Return On Influence* and point to several examples where even celebrity-level influencers couldn't move the needle and create real action through tweeted pleas to their vast audiences.

The reason for this chronic failure is that social media connections begin as *weak relational links*. Sure, we might be willing to help somebody out by clicking a "Like" button or even sending a tweet once in a while for a good cause ... but opening our wallet? No. It normally doesn't happen.

So, going into this project, the request for a donation was a precarious proposition. I knew there was a good chance my appeal could fall flat. Perhaps I would even be publicly embarrassed if I raised nothing. Still, this was a worthy charity in need, so I decided to follow my heart, take a risk, and ask for help.

I wrote a blog post[1] revealing a personal story of my work with an at-risk child and asked, entirely through social media, for a donation to support the sponsoring charity. Even I was surprised at the success—I raised more than $6,000 in one week! I was overwhelmed with joy and pride when I was able to deliver that check to my friends at the charity before Christmas!

On one level, this triumph was inspiring because I realized it never could have happened if I hadn't worked for years building a loyal and engaged social media audience. Without question, all the work I had poured into helping my tribe enabled this achievement. But peeling back this layer reveals another lesson about how truly difficult it is to move an audience toward action.

My charitable request blog post was shared nearly 750 times ... but only 92 people actually made a donation. So in reality, more than 650 people encouraged others to donate without donating anything themselves. Ugh.

This is an example of the immense challenge you face with weak social media links. Many businesses and eager new bloggers make the mistake of equating a large social media audience with power ... and this is just not the case.

Of the 92 people who donated, I had met 80 of them in real life. I had done the work to convert these "weak" audience connections into "strong" personal relationships. The average donation of my strong-link friends was $65. The average donation of my weak-link social media connections was $15.

This means that out of 70,000 followers (at the time), only 12 people on Twitter whom I personally did not know saw the "cold call" tweet asking for help and did something about it. That's a conversion rate of less than two-hundredths of a percent, probably the least effective sales channel you could ever imagine.

But it gets worse.

A couple of social media heavyweights with more than 100,000 followers (and one with more than 500,000 followers!) pitched in to spread the word and raise awareness for the charity. I estimated they generated more than 3 million Twitter impressions. Here's how many donors this intense activity generated: ONE.

So the "celebrity influencer" conversion rate on Twitter was one out of 3 million possible impressions. Sad, but not surprising if you understand how social media audiences work. When I personally asked for a donation, those with an emotional connection built through trust over time—my Alpha Audience—responded to me. When the influencers tweeted, it was like throwing a message in a bottle out into a vast (and apparently lifeless!) ocean. There was just no connection.

While this result may seem depressing, let's return to the actual result and consider the digital dynamics at work. The ability to create content that moves through the Internet is a legitimate source of power. In fact, this is most likely the *only* source of influence I had with any donor! Think of the incredible potential we all possess. From a standing start in 2008, I created a global community who responded to an appeal in one blog post and contributed $6,000 in 48 hours. And that's pretty cool.

Clearly, not all social media fans and followers are created equal. Here are three lessons from this case study:

- The initial audience connections made through social media are weak links that don't drive action on their own.
- Building emotional connections and relationships with these weak links can convert them to a loyal strong link Alpha Audience that you can activate.
- Influence doesn't come from audience size alone.

Don't confuse "activity" with audience

If you think your careful attention to social media analytics, monitoring, and customer relations means you know who is in your Alpha Audience, think again. All that social media data may be misleading you—because it's only showing you a narrow and atypical slice of your customer base.

Research reveals[2] that almost 90 percent of what you hear on social media comes from fewer than 30 percent of the most vocal social media users. And they're fundamentally different from the quieter folks who make up the vast majority of your online audience (and potentially your most important Alpha Audience members). Don't mistake quiet for irrelevant. Even though they're barely posting, the vast majority of lurkers can still be very loyal, sharing your content through more private "dark" modes like text messages, email, and word of mouth.

You can't necessarily use loud social media enthusiasts as a proxy for your customers as a whole. I've learned this time and again—often people who are completely off the social media radar are out there quietly igniting my content, recommending my books, and sharing my ideas in ways I can't measure. I'll cover this phenomenon more thoroughly in Chapter 11.

The awesome power to ignite

With diligence and hard work, every person, and every organization, has the chance to build an audience from scratch these days. The gatekeepers are no longer publishers, editors, and advertising executives on Madison Avenue. We all have the power to build a content-sharing Alpha Audience and create influence on the web through our content.

Not everybody takes advantage of this opportunity. Pew Research reports[3] that just 46 percent of adult Internet users are "creators" who post original photos or videos online. Even fewer—41 percent of adults—have actively transmitted content they've found online.

Unsurprisingly, the digital natives—or Millennial Generation—who will represent 50 percent of the customer base and workforce by 2020, have more aggressive content-sharing habits. Tech experts forecast[4] that the Millennials will lead society into a new world of unprecedented personal disclosure and information-sharing. The digital natives have already embraced sharing through social networks, and this behavior will carry forward even as they age, form families, and move up the economic ladder. This is very good news for you, as you're reading this book in order to understand the Content Code and this culture of social sharing!

The Alpha Audience—the fervent supporters who you can rely on day-in and day-out for support, ignition, and action—are a rare breed. So how do you find more of those people for your business?

Earning reliable reach

Using content as a connection point in the digital world provides an unparalleled, historic opportunity to re-connect with customers and find your Alpha Audience.

For the last 100 years—since the dawn of radio—businesses have been conditioned to broadcast. We couldn't have known it at the time, but when the first commercial radio stations introduced the idea of mass advertising in the 1920s, we were buying a one-way ticket away from the intimate neighborhood market culture that fueled business relationships for centuries. The customer values of trust, loyalty, honor, service, and reputation—the linchpins of long-term business success—were set aside for the intoxicating expediency of advertising.

Today, we're in the post-spin era and those social values are surfacing once again because our customers are telling us so.

Content's role in this new human digital culture is to provide the opportunities—the consistent provocations—to ignite those relational sparks. By providing a drip, drip, drip of communications, you let people know you're there, you care, you're working on something new, and you're solving problems. Through audience-centric messaging you can solve customer problems through your content and immediately establish credibility through your empathy, responsiveness, and authentic helpfulness.

The more the audience engages with your content, the better the chance for a deepening relationship beyond the weak link, perhaps someday blossoming into a two-way relationship … maybe even a relationship based on loyalty and trust.

Marketing's primary goal is to reach consumers at those moments that influence purchasing behavior. Social media is the perfect tool for achieving that goal: It's the only form of marketing that can touch consumers at each and every stage in the buying process, from when they're comparing products right through to the period after a purchase. And ultimately their experience with a brand and potential advocacy influences others.

A recent study from Edison Research[5] showed that 57 percent of American social media users follow a brand on Facebook for no other reason than they have an affinity for the company. And that affinity can create powerful results. The study also shows that one-third of social media users *purchase more* from a brand after they begin to follow them on a social media account.

A study commissioned by Google[6] characterizes the Alpha Audience as the "rapt audience" and says that those who actually engage with brand content have even stronger buying behaviors:

> People who engaged with a brand on social media on a daily basis **were likely to make twice as many purchases** from that brand than someone who engages only monthly. However, socially engaged customers' value to brands goes well beyond purchase. By acting as advocates, these consumers help build brands.
>
> Think of these engaged consumers as your brand advocates. They want to know more about what you have to offer and will champion, broadcast, or amplify on your behalf. In fact, they can significantly increase engagement rates in social media. A brand's advocates account for a significant amount of its earned media: **Brands with high advocate populations generate up to 264% more earned media impressions per campaign than brands with fewer advocates.**
>
> These brand advocates are a rapt audience. When you focus on engaging them through social, at all the moments that matter, you'll turn them into your most valuable customers—loyal ones that don't just buy your products again and again, but encourage others to do the same.

Can you begin to see how critically important your Alpha Audience is? For many companies, it might be their most important asset … but how many of them recognize its power?

Developing a proprietary audience

Jeffery Rohrs, a vice president at Salesforce, wrote a wonderful book called *Audience* that describes the importance of your "proprietary audience." He explains:[7]

> All content marketers are a bit mad. There is more content being produced every day than a person could consume in a lifetime, and yet, we venture forth to do what? Produce more content.
>
> We do so because we're betting on ourselves. We're betting that we can rise above all that other content and reach clients, prospects, and influencers that matter to our company. And so 99 percent of our effort goes into creating amazing content thinking the best content wins. And then we hit "publish" and wait. And wait. And wait.
>
> We collectively suffer from Audience Assumption Disorder, the magical belief that great content magnetically draws audiences we need to succeed. However, publication is not distribution, and a content marketing strategy without an audience development plan is no strategy at all.
>
> There is no magic potion you can drink to make your audience double or triple in size. Rather, there is the hard work of growing your audience with each new piece of content you produce. You must always be building audiences.
>
> Audience development is part and parcel of content marketing, and it's simply not enough to put 1 percent of your effort there. You must create content with your audience and action in mind.

In his book, Rohrs lists three reasons why this important idea has been largely ignored in the marketing community:

- **The concept of proprietary audiences is new.** Prior to the Internet, a proprietary audience was a direct mail database hidden in some huge, distant server. Today proprietary audiences exist inside and outside our databases, and across a vast array of public and private channels.

- **We're typically focused on channel management instead of audience development.** Many companies have Facebook, Twitter, and YouTube strategies, but few have comprehensive Proprietary Audience Development strategies. This leaves marketing pigeon-holed into tactical discussions instead of debates about strategic priorities.

- **Channels are still evolving.** The channels that support proprietary audiences haven't evolved to the point where they provide marketers with simple, consistent ROI measurements. This makes it difficult to provide leadership with more than anecdotal stories of positive audience engagement.

To be clear, an Alpha Audience that is proprietary to your company is not *owned* by your company because no audience is owned. Members can leave any time they want. Whether reading a blog, using a mobile app, or subscribing to an email list, the audience member always has the option to walk away.

While not owned, your core audience can still be proprietary in that the right to communicate with them belongs to a single entity. You.

Digital consultant and author Jay Baer describes this group as the audience of "reliable reach." When you send content into the ether of the web, you never really know where it's going to sink in and take root. But with your Alpha Audience, you know there is a probability they're processing your information and perhaps even acting on it because they've raised their hands and asked for it.

The Alpha Audience profile

A large following on the social channels can make you feel important, but you need to look past the ego-driven need for bigger numbers and devote time to finding and nurturing the only audience who matters, the Alphas.

It's an elite group. A poll of prominent bloggers determined that their Alpha Audience is approximately 5 percent of their total site visitors. Facebook also provided research that shows people considered to be consistent "sharers" of content totaled about 5 percent of a company's total Facebook audience.

So let me introduce you to one of those elite members of my Alpha Audience, Shonali Burke. Shonali is one of the most respected PR professionals in the country and President and CEO of Shonali Burke Consulting. She also teaches at Johns Hopkins University, blogs, speaks, and is an expert in the field of PR measurement.

Shonali and I first became aware of each other through mutual Twitter connections and slowly turned this weak connection into a strong one when we met face to face at a marketing conference. Over the years we collaborated on several projects, she wrote a guest post for my blog, and Shonali hired me for a speaking engagement for one of her client events in New York City.

Shonali also reliably shares my content every single day. In fact, she has become such a fan that she shares the content blindly, setting my content up to share before she even reads it. Consider this for a minute: As a PR professional, she is literally staking her personal reputation on my content with an almost religious sort of faith.

That, my friends, is Alpha. The audience who believes in you at the deepest level. The audience who will be with you to the end. How does an incredibly deep connection like that develop? In her own words:

> One thing I've realized is that if one's business is PR and marketing, then a certain level of social activity is necessary. It's the basic litmus test for service providers in our industry; if prospects don't see us as being social, they are far less likely to consider us as business partners or vendors. So I had to put in place for myself some system of curation similar to what I recommend to clients, or teach about.

> One service I use offers the ability to automatically share people's content. Now, I did not choose to do this for a long time, because not everyone's content is consistent. That's fine; we all have our bad days. But when you are between a rock and a hard place, trying to ensure you curate at least a minimum level of reliable content, you need it to be consistent! That means you have to absolutely trust the quality of content coming from those people.

> That's where your content comes in. You are one of the few people whose content I always share, because I trust you. I've read your blog for so long now, yet

I'm regularly amazed at the smart content you publish—not just from yourself, but from other bloggers. So often I have those, "Why didn't I think of that?" moments after I read your blog. To date, there has not been a single post that made me scratch my head and say, "Meh." I don't always comment because by the time I get to it, you have 76 other comments (!), but I do read. And given that I currently don't have a lot of time to actively source more content, I have to go with content from those I trust: and that group includes you.

You've talked often about how hard you've worked to grow your audience, which is one of the things I like most about your blog {grow} (and you): You share your lessons learned openly and honestly, without minimizing all the hard work you've done. And one of the wonderful consequences of this hard work is that your audience—of which I am one—trusts you.

So, simply put, it comes down to trust, which is one of the keys for businesses grappling with a socialized world. The lesson I learned from you is that building an audience means 1) creating great content that people can trust; 2) curating good content regularly so that people can trust you're not just out to put the spotlight on yourself; 3) participating actively in the social web by giving way more than you get (commenting on other blogs, talking to people and not just at them, and so on).

It makes me consider ... what are we all willing to do to build so much trust that your audience would be willing to share your content blindly?

Trust. There's that word again.
Trust is the launch code for the Alpha Audience rocket.

Trust cements you to the only people who truly matter in your digital world.

The question at the soul of this bond is not "How can you trick, seduce, or coupon your customers into loving you?" It is "How loyal are you to your customers? Do you truly care about *them*?"

The people on the other end of your content aren't just avatars, users, or a target audience. They're human beings who might be suffering, experiencing joy, or simply feel exhausted from caring for their children. And maybe in the moment of connection, they *need* you in some way. What every organization needs before conquering a digital strategy is a human strategy. As I first wrote in *The Tao of Twitter* many years ago, the most successful marketing organizations don't think of themselves as B2B or B2C—they're P2P, striving every day to use these miraculous technologies to connect people to people.

Anybody can figure out ways to generate short-term web traffic. But that's simply a battle for attention you can never win. Let your competitors knock each other out over that. Place your focus in just one place — nurturing a truly loyal audience by running your business in a way that demonstrates mutual respect, gratitude, enduring trust, and … dare I say it? Love. Love is not a word usually embraced by businesses, but how can you create unyielding loyalty without it? Maybe love is the ultimate killer app.

How would your business be transformed if your focus was demonstrating respect, gratitude, and love instead of "traffic?"

This is the digital crossroad, a genuine point of business differentiation today. You can pay people to create great content and then pay people to promote it. Huge companies will escalate and automate their content arms race with breathtaking, epic videos. Eventually computers will be creating excellent content for you with a push of a button. But traffic alone will never, ever create an Alpha Audience.

Building the Alpha Audience through involvement

One of the most powerful ways to create an Alpha Audience of your own is to involve them in the content creation process. Wouldn't you love to be featured on the Facebook page of a company you adore? Wouldn't your passion for a company be inflamed if you were recognized and celebrated by a beloved brand's blog?

With the free social media applications available to nearly everyone, the barriers to creating and publishing content are near zero. Here are some great examples of companies building an Alpha Audience through involvement:

- GoPro[8]: This company sells small video cameras that can be mounted on your body or vehicle (well ... anything really) to capture your activities (like a camera on a helmet worn when skydiving). The tagline "Capture + Share Your World" is the core of its marketing theme. GoPro has become one of the highest-performing brands on YouTube, a calculation based on popularity, time on site, repeat viewership, and shares. When you look through GoPro's YouTube channel, you find videos of everything from people jumping off of roofs to a fireman saving a kitten. GoPro's customer-evangelism strategy is to curate videos from users of its products and broadcast them on YouTube. Not only does GoPro provide a place for authentic advocates to share their most enthralling moments, but its channel is a great way for potential users to see the products in action.

- **Fiskars Scissors:** How do you ignite passion about something as mundane as scissors? With people who love scissors, of course! After about a year of research, Fiskars decided there was an opportunity to create community around a group of people who are passionate about scrapbooking and the tools they use in their hobby. Part of the process involved turning their blog over to customers—four lead "Fiskateers," who sparked a scrapbooking movement that now includes store appearances and conventions. Letting their Alpha Audience lead the content strategy has helped the company dramatically increase positive brand awareness, loyalty and sales.

- **Urban Outfitters**[9]: The retail chain has a successful social media franchise with its #UOOnYou initiative. This campaign invites shoppers to upload and tag photos of themselves wearing branded clothes. The retailer selects photos to feature on its website, Instagram, Tumblr, and product pages. The shopper gets to be a model, other shoppers are inspired by these authentic styles, and for current items, the images link back to OU's e-commerce to make them shoppable.

- **J. Crew:** The retailer noticed that shoppers were posting online photos of one of its most popular Madewell bags—a transport tote—and launched a contest encouraging them to tag the images #totewell for a chance to be featured in company advertising. Even after the contest closed, the most loyal shoppers continued to add photos and artful images to their social profiles and to the brand's various online outlets. Not only did the effort generate content and buzz, but the effort was a good way to identify new Alpha Audience members.

- **Tourism Australia**: Jesse Desjardins calls himself community manager and leader of "the world's largest social media team." His agency receives thousands of fan photo submissions to post on the Tourism Australia Facebook page, one of the largest destination sites in the world. It's not unusual for their amazing photos to get tens of thousands of Likes and shares. Tourism Australia outperforms every other tourism board in the world, and it accomplishes that based on two primary ingredients: user-generated content and community co-creation. Desjardins told me, "We aim to make our audience the hero of our site."

- **Medtronic Diabetes**[10]: A company that manufactures diabetes management products doesn't have a new product to announce every month. It does, however, have a large and active consumer base. People with diabetes want to hear from other people with diabetes. They don't want to hear yet another doctor giving advice in "medical speak." Medtronic taps into that audience and regularly asks for stories, resulting in awareness, news, and sales:
  - Nearly 300 customers have shared stories and photos.
  - Over 80 percent of customers have given Medtronic the rights to use their stories and photos in other media.

- Their "Share Your Story" Facebook app is responsible for a two-to-one increase in return on investment in the effort.

The Escalator Audience model

As you can imagine, the idea of creating an audience of super fans is relevant to almost any industry, but perhaps none has been so intensely studied as sports marketing ... where your job literally depends on creating fans.

In a study on sports fan loyalty,[11] researchers found four stages of "fan-hood:" 1) non-fans; 2) light fans; 3) medium users; and 4) heavy users. Heavy users (the Alpha fans) contribute 80 percent of the revenue to a sports team through ticket sales and merchandise purchases but make up 20 percent or less of the total fan base.

The study proposed distinct marketing strategies aimed at all four user groups with the purpose of moving fans "up the escalator" from one segment to the next. The model emphasizes the importance of satisfying the different needs of each group while promoting movement to the next level.

The strategy for non-fans (or non-consumers, if you like) is devoted entirely to awareness through promotion (which is the focus of Chapter 8). How do you let people know your content exists? What value is there for them to try it? In sports marketing terms, the goal is to get people to attend one game. If they like the experience, chances are they might become a "light consumer."

The next job is identify those who have attended one game—or have had an initial experience with your content—and provide incentives to increase the frequency of their attendance, or in your case, content consumption. Some common techniques in the digital marketing world include offering free content like training videos, webinars, and eBooks in exchange for signing up for a newsletter or subscribing to a content channel. This is the process of turning weak links into stronger links.

As light users in your audience attend additional events or become more regular consumers of your content, they become medium users. These consumers have some interest in you and have probably subscribed to your content channels. Perhaps they even engage in social transmission at this point. The marketing objective with this group is to increase the psychological commitment and get them to identify with a person, brand, or company in a deeper, more emotional way. This is the hardest part: You probably can't get medium consumers to be loyal fans through coupons or eBooks. It takes constant reinforcement that their psychological commitment is acknowledged and rewarded.

There is another aspect to achieving this final stage of fandom … and that's hope.

The Chicago Cubs are iconic in their futility. They have not won a baseball World Series since 1908. And yet they have some of the most dedicated fans in the world, filling Wrigley Field and buying millions in merchandise every losing season.

How is it possible for a team with so little accomplishment to remain so popular? Why would a person emotionally commit themselves—for generations—to a brand associated with futility? Of course part of the answer is emotional attachment but another part is that each spring, the season starts over and every team is on equal footing, at least for a few days. There is always hope; there is always next year. As long as the team owners field a competitive team with a glimmer of hope, the fandom can persist.

There's a lesson here for marketers, too. One famous executive once told me that people keep coming back to his content year after year because they want to be like him. "The vast majority of them will never achieve that," he said. "But as long as I keep giving them hope that yes, it can be done, they keep paying me for my appearances and books."

These are interesting ideas for brands: How do you attract your best customers and most loyal fans by dispensing hope? What would it mean to your business if you methodically attracted an Alpha Audience as loyal as a Cubs fan who will stick with you even through "losing seasons?"

Creating your Alpha Audience: Lessons from the experts

So far, this piece of the Content Code has been about the science of building an audience, but there are also elements of art, perhaps even magic, involved. I asked some of the most successful digital marketers on earth how they do it. What are their secrets to building an actionable, loyal audience who is ready to ignite content?

"Above all, be interesting."
– David Meerman Scott, bestselling author of 10 books including *The New Rules of Marketing and PR*

Many people steeped in the tradition of product advertising naturally feel drawn to prattle on and on about their products and services. But I have news for you. Nobody cares about your products and services (except you). Yes, you heard that right. What people do care about are themselves and how you can solve their problems. People also like to be entertained and to share in something remarkable. In order to have people talk about you and your ideas, you must resist the urge to hype your products and services. Instead, create something interesting for your audience.

"Build the smallest possible audience."
– Seth Godin, marketing author, speaker, and entrepreneur[12]

If your work goes viral, if it gets seen by tens of millions of people, sure you can profit from that. But most of the time, it won't. *Most of the time, you'll aim to delight the masses and you'll fail.*

I'm glad that some people are busy trying to entertain us in a silly way now and then. But it doesn't have to be you doing the entertaining—the odds are stacked against you.

It's so much easier to aim for the smallest possible audience, not the largest, to build long-term value among a trusted, delighted tribe, to create work that matters and stands the test of time.

"Establish a communion of equals."
– Marcus Sheridan, President of The Sales Lion

When it comes to fans and community, there is an essential key I think many people and businesses miss, and here it is: As a content creator, it's NOT your goal to sound smart. Furthermore, it's NOT your goal to put yourself into a higher sphere than that of your audience. Rather, the goal is *communion*. In other words, whatever you say allows them to nod their head and say, "I get it. I see." My success in building communities has been a bi-product of my obsession to find this audience communion, all the while communicating and teaching in a way that establishes the audience as an equal.

"Speak to one person."
– Bernadette Jiwa, author of *Marketing: A Love Story*

Before I sit down to write I think about one person. I don't think about "my audience" as "my audience," I think about a single individual and where they are in their day, in their work, and their life. This practice helps me to understand that I must always respect their time, never take their attention for granted, and always try to provide value. I consider why they should they care that this post exists and why it will matter to them and how I would connect with them if they were sitting right next to me. That's a long way of saying I simply speak to one person.

"Publish with empathy."
– Jonathon Colman, content strategist for Facebook[13]

Many companies put up displays all over the office that are filled with analytics, data, and milestone metrics. But what about feedback from the people using your content? You can display that, too. And while you can build metrics around this feedback (sentiment, influence, comments/hour, etc.), it's even more powerful to display people's actual comments directly on screen. Follow that up by building rapid workflows to solve problems and you're putting empathy into action!

"Don't publish when you 'should.'"
– Scott Stratten, author and President of UnMarketing

Monthly, weekly, daily. In the afternoon. In the morning.

When you ask people how often they should produce content, the answer always ends up being about a spot on the calendar. It used to be biweekly in the old days. Then it became weekly and now it seems to be multiple times a day. Three blog posts a week. Ten tweets a day. Five Instagram pics and one Facebook post an hour. With a picture. And a motivational quote.

But not even once have I, or you, shared a piece of another brand's content because it was "Tuesday at 2 p.m." or because it was a picture with 10 percent text on Facebook. People share emotions. When you evoke that, people react.

The surest way to create the one emotion that doesn't lead to sharing content—apathy—is to send out content because you "should."

"Never take the audience for granted."
– Ann Handley, author of *Everybody Writes* and *Content Rules*, Chief Content Officer of MarketingProfs

I think of my fans and audience in terms of a kind of value exchange that expresses itself in two ways:

First: Is what I'm delivering of value to them? Is the content I'm publishing something useful that will resonate with the people I'm trying to reach? (Or at least ... some of them?) Will it help them? Make them smarter, more informed, inspired, or perhaps entertained?

Second: Is it something that they, in turn, will want to share with their own audiences? Will the value I'm providing delight them enough that they'll want to share what I've shared, in other words?

Inherent in this is an idea that's core to what I believe about any content more generally: That publishing is a privilege and should not be squandered. I started my career in print journalism. And that sensibility from my journalism school days of "No one has to read this," continues to influence and inform what I publish to this day.

"Connecting content, people, and conferences."
– Lee Odden, CEO of TopRank Marketing

A key strategy for converting weak social media links to strong connections for me is attending conferences. I try to get involved as deeply as I can in conferences I attend, even creating unique content for and about these events. I want to create a positive, intelligent and creative experience for the people who are involved so they come to know, "That Lee guy, he does this interesting thing." You know what, in six months or nine months, that turns into something.

The content moves through paid channels, organic channels, through networking, through personal inspiration because we're all creating this really neat thing for a conference that we're all a part of. It's not just some sort of plastic manufactured thing. It really is kind of cool and organic and crowd-sourced. That moves content but I'm also really amazed at how it strengthens connections with the people I get to meet. That has been instrumental in building my audience.

"Don't take the party line."
– Dorie Clark, columnist for *Forbes* and *Harvard Business Review* and author of *Reinventing You* and *Stand Out*

As a former journalist, I try to provide readers with "news"—though instead of the political reporting I did in the past, it's more in the "news you can use" vein. I want to make sure each piece of content has interesting takeaways and that people feel like they've learned something from it. I also try to focus on what I find genuinely interesting.

In everything I write, I try to find the part that's most fascinating and unique, and that's often not the party line, but instead the mistakes and the aftermath and how we grow from them. That's the case with my writing, too, and I try to mention setbacks that I've experienced, like getting turned down for some fellowships, or even how I got started on my book because I was laid off and needed to reinvent myself professionally. This honesty builds trust and audience bonds.

"Connect the community."
– Gini Dietrich, CEO of Arment Dietrich[14]

The community magic doesn't happen when you begin to get comments on your content. It happens when those people begin talking to each other. This isn't something that can be created or forced. It happens organically. But there are things you can do to help the community grow and encourage members to begin building relationships with one another.

If you spend some time online talking to the people who can influence purchase decisions, you can provide the foundation for your community. And, when you do it this way, it becomes much more than engagement.

You build a virtual sales force that isn't on your payroll.

You build goodwill.

You build trust among a group of people who will go to bat for you in a crisis.

You build a referral network.

And you build relationships with human beings who will not only buy from you, but will become your biggest advocates.

Think about it from this perspective: Just like you, prospects, candidates, customers, journalists, and bloggers want to be noticed. They want to know their comments or content resonates. They want you to acknowledge it, share it, and help their voices be heard. Help them do that.

"Be real."
– Joyce Cherrier, health and wellness writer

I look for ways that I can actively be supportive and encouraging to the people in my audience, while providing a positive, not-so-conventional picture of what healthy living is all about. I like to use my own photos, and my personal experiences to create content, as well as share the content of others that I feel will be of benefit. Making my content as personal and applicable to life as possible makes my core audience feel more like old friends who I live and grow with, and I believe that's a key element for any brand.

"Establish a common dream."
– Guy Kawasaki, digital evangelist and author[15]

Want to change the world? Upset the status quo? This takes more than run-of-the-mill relationships. You need to make people dream the same dream that you do.

"Aim for allies, not fans."
– Chris Brogan, CEO of Owner Media Group

Every content creator has a core group of passionate people who are the ones who will buy your books and share your content faithfully. What do you do that attracts and nurtures that core audience of fans?

First, I try not to have fans. I seek allies. Fans are great insofar as they spend money or something, but allies advance the cause. My goal is service, and to be able to serve the folks I have the pleasure to serve, I had to attract them to me. How did I do that? I created information and ideas that resonated with their interests, goals, and desires. In my case, I believe that sharing what I believe draws others who believe similarly to find me. It's like shining the Bat Signal. My goal is to serve, so I have to show "serving suggestions." Once people understand how I can help them, they tend to stick around.

"Give them everything."
– Mark Schaefer, the author of the book you're reading right this minute

I'd like to conclude this chapter with a tale of two famous performers and how one of them taught me how to build my Alpha Audience.

Recently I was fortunate enough to attend two concerts in one week. The first was Art Garfunkel, the legendary singer of Simon and Garfunkel fame. He filled a modest, 1,000-seat hall and performed with a lone guitarist to accompany his iconic voice.

His show was very "me-centric." He complained a lot. He publicly embarrassed a person for opening a door in the back of the auditorium, claiming that it broke his concentration. He told a story of how he humiliated an audience member for texting during his show. We came to hear his famous songs but over the course of 90 minutes, he didn't sing many of them, instead filling time reading his own poetry from note cards. He didn't allow any video or photography, and in an extreme measure, a security officer reprimanded an audience member for taking a selfie before the show even started.

The next night, my wife and I went to see Keith Urban. When he took the stage, 15,000 screaming fans took pictures and videos to celebrate this magical moment, an explosion of sound and light and video images. Some held signs showing the count of how many concerts they had attended or how far they had traveled. At one point Urban walked through the crowd and climbed the arena steps so even people in the highest seats could get a look at him. Along the way, he grabbed phones and posed for selfies, never missing a beat. When he reached the top of the arena, he unstrapped his guitar, signed it, and handed it to a young fan. He played and danced and ran around the stage until he was clearly exhausted ... and then he continued for another 30 minutes to make sure he covered every hit from his songbook and more.

When the show was over and the lights went up, I was amazed to look back and see this global superstar sitting on the end of the stage by himself, dripping with sweat and signing autographs.

And here is what I thought: That man gives his fans EVERYTHING.

The contrast between the two performances was more than a lesson really. It was an inspiration. I left thinking, "That is what I have to do to earn an Alpha Audience. This is what is required in a noisy, competitive world. I have to give my audience everything."

And so do you.

CHAPTER SIX

Borrowing Trust

"Trust is the glue of life."
– Stephen Covey

Before we move on to the next element of the BADASS journey and discover the role of the Heroic Brand in content transmission, let's cover one more important aspect of Alpha Audience development. If you're in a situation where you need marketing traction quickly and you don't have the time it takes to build an Alpha Audience, can you borrow one?

Influence marketing—a plan to find ways for trusted online personalities and experts to become advocates who spread your content—is real, and it's important. As traditional methods of reaching a mass audience dry up or become too competitive, connecting to a "borrowed" audience has become a mainstream marketing strategy.

This is a marvelous, inspiring period of history when you can shed the traditional burdens of authority and build true influence on the web through your own merits. On the web, nobody cares where you went to college or how much money you have. The color of your skin or your body mass index don't keep you from connecting to people on your own terms. Your ability to walk or run or even speak doesn't matter because you can *publish*.

The halls of online influence aren't on Wall Street or Downing Street or Madison Avenue any longer. It's in a café in Berlin. It's in a college classroom in Wisconsin. It's in my office in a little lake-side village in Tennessee where I'm writing this book. It could even be in the chair you're sitting in right now, as long as you have a connected device and an Internet connection!

Companies are learning to identify and tap into the conversations of the new cool kids on the block—the elite few who not only create content, but ignite it.

Like any trend that gets popular quickly, influence marketing is getting stretched and deformed to the point where it's hardly recognizable as a legitimate marketing channel any more. I could fill another book with best and worst practices on influence marketing, but for the focused purpose of this book, I want to emphasize that simply getting important people to share your content doesn't necessarily translate into business success. I'm going to illustrate that point with a story and then, just when you're convinced influence marketing is not for you, I'm going to show you how it is for you. I'm that sneaky. I'm like a cobra hidden in the influence marketing brush.

The downside of viral

Like every new blogger, my dream of success meant getting a business superstar to share my content. I was convinced that validation would change everything and propel me into the sunny skies of Internet fame and fortune. About two years into my blogging career, to my surprise and delight, my dream came true. One of my blog posts was tweeted by marketing superstar Guy Kawasaki, who has a Twitter following roughly the size of France.

As soon as he tweeted the post (on a Friday) my traffic surged, and over the weekend the number of people finding my site was 500 percent greater than the normal rate. Briefly, the Guy-traffic crashed my server and shut down my website. Look at me—I went viral!

When you go viral, you naturally reach a lot of new people outside the comfortable "normal" audience you've built over time. In fact, about 98 percent of the tidal wave of readers over that weekend had never been to the blog before (something that is easily determined through a free analytics program). I had a full weekend of blog tourists!

Guy and his audience had no connection to me, and the new people visiting my site had no reason to stay around after their nanosecond of curiosity had subsided. There was no lasting impact from that traffic spike. As far as I could tell, I didn't even get one new subscriber from the biggest single day ever on my blog, up until that point. Bottom line: There were no discernible business benefits from a superstar igniting my content.

Now that I've moderated your expectations about getting a celebrity to make you famous and successful, it's time for the cobra to strike. Because done well, there are indeed significant benefits you can achieve by igniting content through a "borrowed" audience.

Three types of influencers

Before we get into the tangible benefits of social influence marketing, it's important to know that not all influencers are alike and not all influencers fit every business situation. "Influence" tends to be jammed into one big category when in fact, it's nuanced. Consider this breakdown of three types of influencer and how they might impact a content ignition strategy.

The Celebrity

Kim Kardashian will happily promote your content for $200,000 per tweet. That kind of promotion might seem silly, but it also works ... and it has for more than a century.

According to Thomas Mickey, an advertising and PR industry historian, the first paid celebrity endorsers were probably the stars of P.T. Barnum's circus troupe in the 19th century. "Barnum would have his most popular clowns and entertainers go in advance to the next city," he said. "They would be the faces on the posters and the newspaper ads and it was quite effective. That was the first example of using the power of a character in the media of the day to get a consumer to take action."

When motion pictures and radio were introduced at the turn of the century, technology became the enabler of a new era of celebrity ... and companies loved having these glamorous stars use their products. Celebrity endorsements became commonplace and the most popular program hosts and stars would simply mention the show's sponsor during the broadcast as a means of funding the mass media entertainment. Companies like Proctor and Gamble, Johnson & Johnson, and Kraft built their businesses by funneling millions of dollars into the hands of newly emerging advertising agencies, who eagerly lined up celebrity talent to promote the household products.

The most popular stars of the era, Charlie Chaplin and American baseball star Babe Ruth, endorsed everything from cigarettes to cereal. Ruth's popularity as a pitchman grew to the point that his earnings from advertising far exceeded his salary as an athlete. He was the first individual in history who had to hire a business manager and an accountant just to keep track of all the money he was making from his paid product testimonies.

Today many companies still align themselves with stars. These celebrities have vast audiences and may not even have a deep connection to the products they're promoting. And the cost? Well, for most businesses, it's simply out of reach. Aligning with a celebrity can also be risky, as dozens of brands learned when golf star Tiger Woods' personal life turned scandalous and dominated the news and public opinion.

The Niche Influencer

The niche influencer is the web star most sought-after today by agencies and marketers. These influencers are powerful, self-made industry leaders consistently creating content to establish their authority and expertise. They're tech, food, photography, and car bloggers; the most popular Pinterest stars posting about travel, recipes, and style; and the YouTubers and Viners with millions of followers promoting everything under the sun.

Most of these people are *only* famous because of their content. They may have a medium-to-weak connection to your actual product because they're overwhelmed with requests from every brand in the category. Some mommy bloggers even have agents and six-figure-incomes from their sponsorship deals. It's likely this type of influencer will want to be compensated for supporting you, either directly or indirectly.

Careless marketers might confuse audience size with influence. It's easy for companies to swoon over large numbers of Twitter or Facebook fans (think of the impressions!). But does the niche influencer really influence these followers? Recall the story of "weak links" and my request for charity dollars in Chapter 5. The answer is "no." It's unlikely these folks can legitimately drive action simply because they have a large following without true niche expertise and deep audience connection.

While popular and busy, the true niche celebrities are more accessible than the Hollywood-type influencers and incredible brand synergy can result if you can befriend them and turn them into …

True Advocates

True advocates need no convincing or cajoling. They already love you and can't get enough of whatever you're doing. This is the Alpha Audience that is difficult to find and assemble, but they will probably stick with you forever if you treat them right.

Your true advocates might be the teen who makes videos of her shopping spree at your store, the skateboarder who is never seen without his can of Dr Pepper, or even the quiet fan in the realms of dark social media who worships your work quietly and talks about it with her friends and family.

These are the people who have always been at the heart of word-of-mouth marketing success. Years ago, they were your neighbors, the local power brokers, a labor leader, or the respected business sage. As markets went global, it became more difficult to accurately know who or where these power brokers were, but with the incredible analytics available from Internet data, there are a number of reliable free or low-cost tools available to track influential connections by topic, industry, and region. Combining analytics with observation and insight can provide a historically important opportunity for you to learn about influential new advocates who can help spread your message and your content.

Benefits of borrowed trust

Working on an influencer outreach plan to ignite content is essential to many businesses today and certainly a strategy that can provide rapid, repeatable, and sustainable benefits. Here are some of the deliverables that can come from influencer outreach:

- **Authentic advocacy:** If you can establish a long-term connection with an influencer that results in a strong relationship and true advocacy, there is probably no other more effective way to ignite your ideas and products. For example, Chobani Yogurt does an excellent job reaching out to influencers in an authentic and helpful way. One friend has repeatedly referred to the brand in case studies, recommendations, and blog posts simply because he has truly come to love the brand.

- **Fast traction:** One of the challenges of building an Alpha Audience is that it takes time—often a long time. If you're starting from scratch and don't have the time, getting your message out through a trusted influencer can potentially give your business a jolt in a hurry. Robert Scoble is one of the most famous tech bloggers in the world. A few years ago, he quadrupled the traffic to a start-up company's site with one blog post—over a Christmas weekend!

- **Social proof:** Chapter 9 explores the idea of validation through association, or *social proof*. Having your brand associated with a well-known authority can help augment your reputation instantly. If they're trusted, then you're trusted.

- **Awareness:** When Ford launched the Fiesta brand, they created a social media "Fiesta Movement." One hundred digital influencers were selected and given the keys to a car for six months. These Fiesta agents completed monthly challenges, posted videos, and blogged about their experiences. The campaign, masterminded by Scott Monty, was spectacularly successful. By using social influencers, Ford exposed the Fiesta name to a new generation of users (the name had been defunct in the U.S. for more than a decade). The campaign gained 6.2 million YouTube views, 750,000 Flickr views, and 40 million Twitter impressions. Most importantly, it singlehandedly brought top-of-mind awareness for the Fiesta to a key demographic—132,000 drivers signed up for updates on the car and more than 6,000 preordered the automobile, an exceptionally strong showing for a new economy car.

- **Access to new channels:** In the past few years, new channels have emerged that provide access to valuable niche demographics. The problem is, how does a company build and maintain audiences rapidly on every one of those platforms? Juan Pablo Zurita is a business-savvy teen heartthrob who built a massive Alpha Audience on Vine and Snapchat through his hilarious and engaging videos. Brands like Coke are gaining exposure in these highly desirable niches by sponsoring him and accessing his audience of 1 million adoring fans.

- **New markets exposure:** Combining products with influencers can ignite interest from new customer groups. When Audi introduced a new A8 sedan into the American market, it held special influencer events across the nation targeted at well-known tech and design bloggers instead of the traditional automotive crowd. They figured their revolutionary car would appeal to these diverse thought leaders, and the result was massive coverage that connected them with new audiences very quickly.

- **Cost-effective reach:** If your goal is exposure, in most cases, influencer outreach provides "impressions" at a cost that is more favorable than traditional advertising.

- **Feedback loop:** Testing ideas with influencers and their audiences can be an efficient way to rapidly assess new products and content ideas.

So influence marketing has a lot of potential benefits, but it relies on a strategic, methodical practice, not blind luck. Building an audience of influencers takes time, too.

Groove, a company that provides help desk software, is a perfect example of executing an influencer strategy with precision. They were a start-up company with literally no audience—and no time to build an audience—so they relied on borrowing the audiences of others. The result? 5,000 new blog subscribers in five weeks. Here's how they did it:[1]

1.Build the influencer list. The company carefully considered which potential influencers connected to their target audience (web start-ups and small businesses) and which of those leaders would be able to get true value from their content and service. This is a critical step. Most influencers are deluged with spammy requests for their help, so doing careful research up front gives you the best shot at success.

2. Forge relationships. Influencers may hold the keys to the audience kingdom, but simply making a cold pitch doesn't work. Groove embarked on a plan to use the social networks to connect with them and move beyond the relational weak link. Their plan included tweets, blog comments, blog post shares, and emails. Here are other ways to engage with influencers:

- Ask for a quote you'll use in your article.
- Re-tweet them consistently.
- Provide them with a recommendation on LinkedIn.
- Interview them for a video or podcast.
- Ask them for feedback on an idea.

- Link to something they wrote about (they will generally see this "pingback").

3. The Ask (part 1). By this time, the people from Groove were on the radar of their target influencers and it was time to make a move. But they didn't ask for a favor. They asked for help—a subtle yet important difference. Most people have a hard time saying "no" to an honest request for help. This plea included a link to their site, a request for feedback, and emphasis on potential mutual benefits. Using this technique, Groove earned an 83 percent positive response rate from the influencers. "Help" is a more benign ask, and more importantly, it helped Groove start real back-and-forth conversations with industry experts.

4. The Ask (part 2). Now that the company was ready to launch their blog, they needed a push from their new influencer friends. Since this group had been involved in providing feedback to the Groove team, they had a built-in stake in the company's success. Groove sent these new advocates a link to the first blog post with a request for help promoting it.

5. Results! Not only did most influencers promote the post, but almost all of them also commented on the new blog. This level of response provided proof to new visitors that the blog (and company) had traction. In 24 hours Groove had acquired 1,000 blog subscribers, and by following up with consistent, high-quality content, they attracted more than 5,000 subscribers and 535 trial sign-ups through five weeks of blogging efforts.

In this case, Groove methodically built relationships with influencers that led to measurable success. But there was another force at work here, too—the powerful, magnetic attraction of involving key audience members in your content creation and transmission.

As influence marketing has rapidly gained acceptance as a mainstream marketing competency, the number of options for how to succeed in this space have proliferated.

Building an internal competency

Dozens of new platforms have emerged to help you build your own influencer list, connect with them, and nurture an Alpha Audience relationship. Like our friends at Groove, with the right resources and a little elbow grease, there's no reason that even a small business can't figure this out and manage the process themselves. In fact, a DIY approach might provide an advantage over agency outsourcing because influencers appreciate the direct connection with key members of a company. Remember, you're building long-term relationships, not running a campaign that fluctuates with a quarterly budget.

The most challenging part of the process is finding and nurturing the right advocates, especially in a very large company with thousands or millions of customers. A thought leader in this enterprise-influencer space is Shree Dandekar, Senior Director of Product Management, BI Analytics for Dell. Dandekar's philosophy is that creating advocacy means leading customers on a journey, and that customer journey involves multiple touch points with content serving as the ignition at each intersection.

While it's important to understand, measure, and shape social influence, it can also be extremely complicated for a large company. To achieve success on a massive scale, you need an assist from software that automates the collection, filtering, and analysis of all that data.

"We use social analytics software based on Dell patented technology and integrate it into all aspects of our business," Dandekar said. "Even though we assess more than 1.5 million online conversations annually, we can drill down to very granular feedback in real time."

This patented content assessment engine scores 150 different conversation categories on an 11-point sentiment scale, enabling Dell and its customers to make sense of the vast amount of customer feedback and react immediately. The company has also developed metrics to help them find the most important advocates and accurately know where they are on their customer journey, allowing Dell to tailor their content, messages, and responses to each influencer.

"Essentially we're scaling human connection," he said. "It's how we create a company-wide strategy of customer centricity and direct feedback. Since the software is constantly updating in real-time, we can accelerate customer feedback and our response times. Once you've started to engage with your influencers you can't abruptly stop that communication. It's crucial to have the infrastructure in place to be able to keep those relationships moving forward."

Dandekar said another advantage of this approach is that feedback from influencers can be shared with all appropriate departments, including product development, quality assurance, customer care, corporate communications, and influencer relations.

Out-source influencer relations

In research I spearheaded for a client, we found that 85 percent of all U.S. advertising and PR agencies now offer some sort of influencer outreach program for their customers. Of that number, only a very small group—generally the largest agencies—have developed their own proprietary methods to identify influencers. Most agencies are using common software programs and measurement practices that are available to anyone.

One danger in using an agency is that in a very real sense you're outsourcing a critical business relationship. If you count on an outside company to develop these relationships for you, you risk losing those connections if the agency decides not to renew your contract. In fact, they could take your hard-earned influencers to a competitor.

On the other hand, the benefit of outsourcing is that many agencies now have skilled staff members who can help you get up and running effectively and quickly so you can avoid a lengthy learning curve. Out-sourcing can be particularly effective in a company that is resource-constrained, or as a bridge to building an internal competency.

Hybrid/subscription approach

A hybrid approach is to subscribe to a sophisticated influence software service like Appinions. Appinions has patented technology that scans the web to assess millions of online publishing platforms and find your most relevant online thought leaders, sliced and diced by many detailed variables. These services aren't inexpensive, but they can save you months of work. If influencer connections are key to your success, software like this might be the edge you need to get up to speed quickly and develop a competitive advantage.

While reading this chapter, it may have occurred to you that it could be fun to be on the other side of the relationship and become an influencer yourself. Well, then. You're going to love the next chapter in our content ignition adventure! Have you thought about becoming a Heroic Brand?

CHAPTER SEVEN

The Heroic Brand

"When people believe that what you believe is what they believe, they turn you into a belief." – Michael Bassey Johnson

I n Chapter 1, I shared a story about content ignition—blogger and entrepreneur Chris Brogan's 37-word blog post about talking over slides that went viral. This example doesn't seem to follow any of the guidelines I've covered in The Content Code so far. Why did this modest snippet of non-epic content set off a social sharing firestorm?

It had nothing to do with the emotion of the content, clever headlines, shareability tricks, or the Alpha Audience, did it? *But it had everything to do with the individual who created that content.* This chapter explains how content can ignite simply because of who you are. It's the "B" in the BADASS formula—your Brand.

Every person reading this book has a personal brand based on what people believe about you (not to be confused with the facts about you!). Do people believe you to be quirky, dependable, passionate, creative, funny, driven, or shy? Those impressions eventually coalesce to form your brand. The impressions may vary slightly from person to person depending on how well they know you and your company, but there are likely general themes that form the foundation of your perceived brand across your audience.

Everything you say online—and everything you don't say—contributes to the story about you that plays in people's heads. While everyone has a personal brand, not everybody has a *Heroic Brand* that can put content sharing on auto-pilot. And Chris Brogan has a Heroic Brand. Here's the connection between his powerful online persona and content ignition, in his own words:

> "Some people share content just because they believe in you and what you stand for. I believe there are three core elements of personal branding, at least for me, and they are very intertwined and related.

> "First, I'm exactly who I am no matter if you talk with me online, offline, in the lobby of a hotel, or before/during/after my time on stage. I think that an integrated (and true to life) persona is vital. People can no longer get away with being someone they're not. It just doesn't work. At least not for long.

> "Second, I believe that connecting with others and serving them is one of the most important parts of personal branding. That's a mistake most people make. Your brand isn't exactly about you. It's about how others experience you. So I work hard to connect, to respond, to be available, and to show people I'm just like them for the most part.

"Finally, personal branding and connecting with people is about making information portable enough that others can make it their own. I say two or three things over and over: Give your ideas handles (meaning, make it easy for others to take the ideas with them). Everything I do is steal-enabled (as much as I dislike plagiarism, I love when people take my ideas and run with them—with a little credit). Brevity and simplicity are gold (most often, people try to convolute their ideas to make them seem more important than they are). To be simple is to be more open and honest."

In the Alpha Audience chapter, Brogan characterizes his core audience as "allies" instead of fans. Are there principles to building this steadfast allegiance that anyone can learn and activate? How does a person, company, or brand inspire fanaticism to the point where it almost doesn't matter what content you create? How do you ensure it ignites because of who you are?

The Heroic Brand and the magic of reciprocity[1]

A common but often ignored driver of both brand-building and social transmission is reciprocity, or the obligation to return favors. Indeed, whatever power structure exists on the social web, it's often built on a foundation of subtle indebtedness, an ability to create influence through an economy of favors. Online, as in the real world, if somebody does us a favor, we feel a powerful obligation to repay the debt. Sociologists such as Alvin Gouldner report that there is no human society that doesn't subscribe to this rule.

But a difference between indebtedness in the "real world" and on the Internet is that it can be created on the social web with little or no effort, even by just clicking a "Like" button on Facebook, or retweeting a message for a friend. In these cases, expending very little effort can still create an expectation that if "I moved your content, you need to move mine."

"Much influence on the social web is built on a promised return of favors," said Tom Webster, vice president of Edison Research. "We coexist every day on small favors ... like if you retweet this, I'll retweet yours. I'll like your page if you'll like mine. The effort to accomplish these things is low—so they are easily done."

"To be more effective at promoting your content, you first need to become more effective at promoting other people's content," said Internet strategist Carol Lynn Rivera.[2] "The Internet is a relationship economy. You have to give to get. Very few bloggers or businesses are at a level where they will have their content read and shared if they are absent from the process.

"What that means is that you need to be involved in getting to know people—other bloggers and business people, commenters, subscribers, Twitter and Facebook and even Pinterest connections. Everyone. When you build those relationships and when you share, promote, and comment on other people's work in a way that adds genuine value, then your presence will be known and appreciated and the sharing will be reciprocated. So I guess the bottom line is that if you want more success promoting your content then you have to stop focusing on promoting your content. Refocus your efforts on others."

Perhaps the most famous purveyor of reciprocity is author and media mogul Gary Vaynerchuk, who emphasizes a simple formula: "give, give, give, give, then ask." (Or his latest iteration: "jab, jab, jab, right hook.") This is reciprocity in action—trading in on favors to build social capital.

Gary's signature move is asking people through Twitter what he can do to help them—and he has done some pretty crazy things. Sending a pie overnight. Shipping bottles of hot sauce to someone who had run out. Delivering a person's favorite hamburger just because she asked.

This might seem like a random way to run a media consulting business unless you understand the strong need we have to fulfill an obligation. Getting something seemingly for free has such an impact because we're psychologically obsessed with repaying that favor; we don't feel that we *should* repay, but rather we feel *compelled* to repay.

Yes, some people may take advantage of Gary's apparent generosity, but most of the time, the odds of reciprocity—via favors, gifts, invitations, and even tweets—are in his favor.

Expectations of reciprocity are amplified on the social web. There is a quid-pro-quo economy that drives a constant state of obligation. When you get down to it, you create authority that isn't really earned—you bargain for it.

Vaynerchuk bluntly claims his strategy is to "guilt people into buying stuff."[3] Can that work as a long-term strategy? Is that building loyalty? A community? Is he building long-lasting relationships that lead to real business, or a house of cards built on stunts?

Vaynerchuk found a way to monetize his guilt trips by building something that can last. But sometimes breaking the cycle of reciprocity also has its place. Being selfless has a powerful multiplying effect on the social web because good deeds aren't just experienced by the recipient, but potentially countless others who observe the act, or perhaps hear about it.

Ultimately, reciprocity can create both long-term influence and short-term leverage. Being authentically helpful and giving of your time and talent without an expectation of reward can have a multiplying effect as your goodwill is observed and noted by others. And connection and influence moves content.

Beyond buying and into "believing"

The process of creating a heroic brand ultimately must move beyond the transactional expediency of reciprocity. We also create emotional connections with our favorite bloggers, YouTubers, Pinterest pinners, and even companies because they stand for something we believe in.

You see, content is much more than a sales tool, a marketing strategy, or the engine behind an SEO machine. The ability to publish anything, anywhere, anytime, for all the world to see is a valuable opportunity to establish connection with your audiences in an intimate way, in a truly heroic way.

We have always bought from those we knew and trusted. Heroic brands in the year 1900 might have been the doctor who travelled through the night by horse to heal a sick child, a banker who bent the rules to help a customer in desperate need, or a carpenter who was willing to work for scraps of wood because a customer's cash was tight. We worked with people we believed in, and we stuck with them.

In our hearts, we still want that, but businesses might have lost that focus in a world where it's so easy to pump up quarterly sales with a coupon or a quick TV promotion. With the drip, drip, drip of consistent content, you can recapture the personal connection at the heart of the heroic brand.

A person who deeply understands this intimate connection is Bernadette Jiwa, an acclaimed marketing consultant and author. "Like many content creators I think generosity is the key to standing apart," she said. "My aim has been to give without expecting in return.

"I don't accept sponsorship or paid links. I think people like the non-salesy approach; they trust that I am here to give first, last, and always. That's enabled me to build a lot of trust. When you give from a place of not taking, people really do want to give back.

"I write about understanding your customer's worldview, about that being the secret to changing how people feel and the foundation of a great brand story," Jiwa said. "You either believe this or you don't. There is no middle ground. I think standing for something in this way means that people like you, those who share the same values, want to join you."

The one-way hero

Much of the time, this intimate, content-earned connection isn't two-way. One man wrote me, "I saw you give a speech three years ago and have followed your blog ever since. I have never reached out to you before, but I just wanted to let you know that I am a fan and I am sharing your content in my workplace almost every day. We even use your ideas in our customer meetings. I wanted to let you how much I have learned from you, how much I appreciate your integrity and what you stand for in this crazy business world."

Through the magic of my content alone I was able to form a meaningful, personal connection with a person I've never heard of, a man who lived on the other side of the world, in fact. How could this have happened in another age?

This opportunity exists for everyone. It doesn't matter if you have a college degree, an important job title, a fancy house, or political connections. Those trappings of power no longer matter. You can be a hero to your audience through your sincere hard work, passion, and dedication to your content.

Through your content you not only show what you sell, but *who you are*. This is the difference between being a content producer and taking the first step toward becoming a Heroic Brand. For example, sports fans or people working on political campaigns don't see themselves as buying into a product. They belong to a larger movement. Such an ideal aligns with an individual's sense of self and drives him or her to evangelize the team, product, or person with almost blind dedication.

"The inspired leaders and the inspired organizations, regardless of size and industry, all think and act from the inside out," said author Simon Sinek.[4] "However, most people sell, market, and communicate from the outside in. Consider the tagline 'We make great cars through great research.' It's not terribly inspiring. The best companies market from deep within their development process using their inner why and speaking directly to the heart of the foundation."

Sinek refers to Steve Jobs, who once commented that his most hated words were "branding" and "marketing." Former Apple marketing vice president Allison Johnson explained that in the late Apple CEO's mind, "people associated brands with television advertising and commercials and artificial things. The most important thing was people's relationship to the product. So any time we said 'brand' it was a dirty word.

"Marketing is when you have to sell to somebody," Johnson said. "If you aren't providing value, if you're not educating them about the product, if you're not helping them get the most out of the product, you're selling. And you shouldn't be in that mode."

Can any person or company become a Heroic Brand?

One of the most progressive and honest commentators in marketing today is Jay Baer. Although well-known as a consultant, speaker, and author of the best-selling book *Youtility*, Jay is also a trusted voice of reason in the digital cacophony. We had a great debate on this question: Can anyone get to a point where people share your content just because of who you are? His valuable insight follows:

> "Every time I publish a blog post, approximately 125 people tweet it instantly using some sort of automation protocol. It's gratifying to be so trusted that this group believes it is in their best interest to automatically redistribute what I write. But I also find it frightening, and it's not something I would ever do myself.

> "While I certainly try to create appropriate content every time I open the laptop to write, I know that some content is better than other content, the same way that not every batch of pulled pork is your tastiest, and not every workout achieves a personal best. By automatically sharing all of my content, this group is indirectly saying that my C game is still meritorious. That's amazing to me, especially considering my attitudes could change, I could just be wrong (happens all the time), my blog could be hacked, and any number of other calamities could occur that would cause

something I publish to be far below an acceptable standard.

"But that's the power of content curation as a brand-builder. These people build their brands partially by sharing my stuff, and I build my brand partially because they are sharing my stuff (and I, in turn, am sharing stuff created by other people). It's a curation circle, and as someone who has greatly benefitted from that trend, I certainly will not indict it universally.

"This is similar to how some musicians, actors, and authors benefit from a consistent track record. If a new Radiohead album comes out, I'm buying it, period. I'll see every Jennifer Lawrence movie. I'll read every Bill Bryson book. What we see in social media is just a smaller and less consequential version of this dynamic, accompanied by greatly reduced economic stakes since social sharing requires investment of trust capital, rather than the actual currency used to purchase movie tickets, digital downloads, or books.

"I believe the central question here is nature versus nurture. Can any person with smarts, relevant expertise, and an unyielding commitment create relationships create a brand that would cause other people to automatically share their work? I think the answer is yes ... and no.

"I fully believe that just about anybody can achieve a level of success by creating and sharing consistently good content about topics people care about, while also being wise and diligent about content amplification and promotion. From scratch, you can make someone good at content. However, can you take the same person under the same conditions and coach them in a way that they have what you call a 'heroic brand?' I

THE CONTENT CODE | 153

don't think so, or at least I've never been able to do it for anyone other than myself.

"I think this is because content-driven success is the same as music, or art, or acting, or comedy, or golf, or any endeavor where you're competing as an individual. Competency can be learned. But the distance from competency to the next level (heroic brand, in this case) is actually farther than the distance from zero to competency. You can pick up golf for the first time at the age of 45, put a ton of time and effort and money into it, and learn how to be a decent golfer. You can learn to play piano credibly. You can learn to paint. You can become a strong content creator who is a trusted information resource. But, can you just set your mind to it and end up as a professional golfer? Unlikely. Can you just decide to play piano and end up on the concert stage? Unlikely. At some point, an aptitude layer, or the 'it factor' kicks in, and that's what allows people to move from very good to the highest level. That aptitude layer is what builds a heroic brand.

"Gary Vaynerchuk is a very smart guy. But most of the time he's not saying anything different about business and social media than anyone else. However, he has a style and a personality that sets him apart— charisma that most people don't have. And it matters. Is Jennifer Lawrence the very best actress of her generation? She's good, probably not the best. But, she is extremely likable in a way that most people (especially celebs) are not. It sets her apart, and it matters. Am I any smarter than most people creating marketing content and dispensing business advice for a living? No. But, I'm a better writer than average, I'm a better headline writer than most, I'm a better speaker than some, I'm consistent like rain in Seattle, and for reasons I don't fully understand people tend to like me and want to support me.

"You can learn to be good. But the It Factor determines if you'll transcend that. And of course, your 'it' is totally circumstantial and occupationally specific. Would Jennifer Lawrence be the most likable college administrator? I doubt it. Would I be successful in music? Probably not, because my 'aw shucks' thing that works in business wouldn't be a cool enough vibe to translate to 'it' in that world.

"So, the key to building a heroic brand with content isn't just having the It Factor, because I think everyone probably has it in some way. The key is to figure out in which world or subculture your version of 'it' is valued, and ply your trade there. Find the place where who you are and how you communicate and comport yourself represents something approaching the ideal for that subculture. That's the place where your own version of the It Factor will take you from competent to a heroic brand."

Stepping toward the Heroic Brand

If you work for a large company, at this point, you might be thinking, "What does this have to do with me? This is out of my hands. An advertising agency does all this stuff."

The best-managed companies are pushing hard to humanize themselves and emphasize the P2P (people-to-people) factor. They realize that building online relationships can't be a campaign that fluctuates with the annual budget. The best brands recognize that the nature of marketing has fundamentally changed because the expectations of consumers have changed. They're people who want to be treated like people, not "targets."

I love this perspective from Linda Boff, GE's executive director of global brand marketing.[5] "Most people still associate our brand with appliances and lighting," she said. "But that's a very, very small part of GE. We are early adopters; we are a brand that is about innovation, invention, discovering things. And early adopters are the kind of people we want to be talking to, the kind of people who might want to work at GE, or partner with us, or invest with us. And we want to humanize the company. We want to throw open the doors and behave the way a person behaves."

So you see, building a human and heroic brand is important no matter the size of your company.

This chapter has covered a lot of ground, from the aptitude layer to reciprocity, from influence to the It Factor. Let's put it all together and codify some practical steps to finding and releasing your inner hero.

1. Establish congruity.

There are a number of readers of my blog who share it with their audiences almost every day. One of them is the media-savvy Brooke Ballard, founder of B Squared Media in New York. She recently told me why she makes the decision to share my content so regularly:

> "My relationship with the author matters. I started to get to know about you through your blog, as you serve up little slices of life to your readers. We hear about your travels, your life, and your family ... and if users are following you on social, they get other tantalizing bites through actual pictures of those things. An entire portrait is painted—providing insight to who you really are. Maybe it's my own love of psychographics and being human that leads to that connec-

tion, but very few people let others in the way you do— with true transparency.

"For me, tone also has something to do with it," Ballard continued. "Your tone is similar to mine. You're firm in your beliefs and teachings, but fair when others comment and disagree. You simply add another layer to the lesson. This helps me share your content because I trust you. I know my audience will learn something, they won't be scolded for having a different viewpoint, and they will be encouraged to elaborate when they have questions or want to know more. Your willingness to respond to comments on your posts helps people connect to you in a meaningful and personal way."

Nearly every expert I interviewed for this book mentioned the importance of honesty, trust, and congruity as the centerpiece of their brand strategy. Remember that a decision to share content isn't trivial. It's an extension of self-identity. We feel better sharing content from those we know and trust. The only way to establish that through your content is to have the courage to reveal yourself and connect to people in an authentic and meaningful way.

2. Be prepared to do the work.

If you study many of the great heroes in business, sports, entertainment, or any other field, you'll find that they put in an incredible amount of work. If you're a business that wants to rise above and capture the hearts of a passionate audience, you're going to have to exert the effort to get there.

If you want to be at the top of your field, you can't dabble in it. You have to approach this with an Olympian's dedication. Olympic athletes practice their sports for hours every day without fail. Are you willing to put in the work?

3. Find your It Factor.

It's improbable that you're a true celebrity. If you are, I would certainly like to hear about it so I can tell my mother. It's also improbable that you'll ever become a true celebrity. However, it's certainly possible for you to have a heroic brand within your industry niche.

It's hard for people to talk about this and perhaps even harder to define it, but great leaders in every field stay ahead by doing things differently. How can you own an area by applying new and creative ideas to tired ways of doing business?

In the movies, our favorite heroes have abundant courage. We love them even more if we see them overcoming adversity to achieve their status (Batman, Superman, and Spiderman were all orphans!). There is an important link between content, brand, and courage.

To stand out on the web you need to be original ... and to be original you have only one choice—find the courage to dig down deep and infuse your content with a bit of your personality, a bit of your own creativity. You have no competitors. There is only one you.

4. Where's the break?

Most people who are at hero status had a break along the way, usually through an established mentor who saw potential in them and was willing to help. Don't be afraid to network and ask for help, especially if you have relationships with established heroes in the field.

5. Become a servant leader.

While exchanging favors through reciprocity is a powerful engine on the web, I think a better view of "giving" as a leadership strategy is expressed by author and entrepreneur James Altucher[6] as he reflected on the common thread among 80 "heroic" people he interviewed on his podcast.

"I don't think I spoke to a single person who believed in setting personal goals," he said. "But 100 percent of the people I spoke to wanted to solve a problem for the many. It doesn't matter how you give each day. It doesn't even matter how much. But everyone wanted to give and eventually they were given back.

"Nobody succeeded with just a great idea. Everyone succeeded because they built networks within networks of connections, friends, colleagues...all striving toward their own personal goals, all trusting each other, and working together to help each other succeed. This is what happens only over time. This is why giving creates a bigger world because you can never predict what will happen years later."

Another common theme among marketing leaders I interviewed was elevating your audience. "The key to nurturing your own audience and elevating your own brand is, ironically, elevating those around you," said Ann Handley of Marketing Profs. "This starts with data: Knowing who your audience is, and where they are, and what you can offer that's most of value, and how you might offer it.

"But it continues with listening (reading what they write, following them, hearing what most resonates), engaging (sharing what they write, commenting, and sometimes challenging), and inviting them to share their thoughts and ideas with our community."

With great content and an engaged Alpha Audience backing you up, becoming a true servant leader is probably the single-most powerful creator of "heroic" connection and influence on the web.

6. Market yourself.[7]

You've found your niche, toiled tirelessly at your craft, and networked with the best in the business. The work is just beginning because none of this matters if you're not known. The trick is, how do you do promote yourself and not come across as a jerk?

The first step is understanding the true value of self-promotion. Sure, you have a self-interest in the activity, but when done the right way and not seen as merely transactional, it can also help others know what talents and knowledge you have that can help them.

The next step is to focus on facts, not brags. No one can argue if you say that you've been blogging for more than a decade, or that you have a degree from Michigan State University. But they can argue plenty if you call yourself a "social media expert." Whatever your field, it's fine if other people want to christen you an expert, but it's presumptuous to do it yourself, and you risk a great deal of blowback.

Third, demonstrate your expertise with actions and stories, not words. Saying "I'm great at pitching investors" sounds egotistical. But sharing a compelling tale of how you rounded up seed funding allows others to deduce your skill without making it explicit. Also, research shows[8] that when listeners are exposed to your stories, many more sections of their brains light up; they're literally immersed in the moment with you, making a far deeper impression. They may hear your words if you say you're awesome, but telling them a story allows them to feel it for themselves.

There is power in humility. According to research published in *Psychology Today*,[9] the overwhelming emotion people feel when viewing their Facebook timeline is jealousy. In a world where we always present our shiny best selves, it's easy for feelings of jealousy to become inflamed. It's fine to present information about your successes, but keep in mind that every brag may also elicit feelings of inadequacy from your audience.

Another factor to consider when promoting yourself is cultural sensitivity. In a speech I gave to an audience in a Baltic country, I mentioned that I had just come from England where I lectured at Oxford University. I thought this was a point of interest but also a way to quickly establish credibility with an audience who was unfamiliar with me. After the speech, one person told me how he admired the boldness of the Americans—people in their country appreciated humility and would never make such a comment in public! A week later I gave a talk to a group of Chinese MBA students and was told to leave humility at the door—I needed to list my accomplishments upfront to establish my "worthiness" with this group. Viva diversity!

7. Connect in a human way.

People want to know who you are and what you stand for.

A "publisher as human" role model is author and entrepreneur Gini Dietrich. "The biggest thing that has worked for me is I let people know they're heard," Dietrich said. "Even if they disagree with me, I always thank them for their input and try to continue the conversation. I always say that if you stroke the egos of the people who spend time with you, they'll always repay you in gold. It may sound disingenuous—stroke their egos—but I mean it in a very sincere and caring way. Pay attention to what people care about. Let them know you are present and attentive.

"People are choosing to spend their precious time with your content. Spend time in return getting to know them and remember the little things that make a difference."

Although "being human" might seem like common sense, it's not. Too often organizations get tied up in regulations, legal overview, advertising protocol, or simply a conservative corporate culture and have been removed from the customer relationship.

"When I follow someone back or I say hello or thanks for retweeting," said Ann Handley, "or I respond and retweet *them* ... the action is often met with surprise. As in, 'Wow! You're a real person!' That's kind of sad, isn't it? Expectations are so low for many of us that when a 'brand' engages with real conversation and real emotion, it's a kind of shock."

What would you think of a company who unexpectedly delighted you with this message: "We know you're a Manchester United fan. We saw this awesome photo from the match yesterday and wanted to share the link with you." That's the kind of message you would get from a friend. That's the kind of message that makes you a hero.

When most people think of moving content, they think of promotion and advertising. That's the next step in The Content Code ...

CHAPTER EIGHT

Distribution, Advertising, Promotion, and SEO

"Without promotion, something terrible happens...nothing!"
– P.T. Barnum

I n today's competitive online world, even the best content may not rise to the top on its own. Sometimes it needs a little nudge. This chapter is all about nudging your content and brand forward through something other than organic distribution channels.

To assemble something meaningful, actionable, and accessible on these broad topics, I'll take a strategic view with this chapter. Rather than diving into niche services and tactics that will be out of date in a year, I focus on imperatives that will be as relevant years from now as they are today. Let's take another step toward unlocking the Content Code with an assessment of alternative methods of igniting your content, the "D" in your BADASS strategy—Distribution, Promotion, Advertising, and SEO.

Distribution

Distribution is one of the most overlooked components of the Content Code and yet an opportunity brimming with potential.

Mitch Joel, president of Mirum (one of the largest digital marketing firms in the world), explains how finding new distribution outlets transformed his content efforts. "I've been blogging for well over a decade, almost every day. I've produced something like 4,000 entries. I've built an audience over that time but a couple years ago I noticed it was getting harder and harder to attract new people to the content. It wasn't necessarily me or what I was writing, although you can't rule that out as a factor, but what happened is true Content Shock. There's simply too much content and the content is so great it's hard for anything to rise.

"The strategy I took to reach a new audience was to go beyond my walled garden—the framework of the blog, my podcast, the social channels like Facebook and Twitter—and start writing in other channels. Huffington Post. INC Magazine. Harvard Business Review. A book.

"What I quickly realized is that by taking quality content and making it work for another platform—and a relevant new audience—I was driving attention back to my home site and content, and ultimately the work that we are doing at our agency. The results to me were astounding. It showed up in the analytics, but it also brought a new energy and enthusiasm to the audience who was consuming my content. I realized that I can't keep all of my content in one place. I need to get in the hands of people wherever they are.

"I look at a lot of content that brands are producing and it's fantastic," Joel continued. "And I often wonder why they would not embark on the same kind of strategy. I think if they could tweak that content and submit it to other channels— authentically, not some part of a PR spin—they could build audiences on other major platforms they would not normally access. That would be profoundly powerful. I think this will happen—brands not necessarily paying to spread their content, but creating work so excellent that it is eagerly picked up and shared by mainstream media."

This type of *earned media*—validation by powerful third party sites—is the most important and effective method to market your content, attract relevant new audience members, and build credibility as a content creator. Anything a brand or marketer says is immediately suspect, but amplification from trusted third parties is a valuable win for content ignition with potentially far-reaching impacts.

Let's break this type of distribution down into some actionable ideas:

1. Plan for multi-channel content.

As Mitch Joel states, a look outside the "walled garden" can produce astounding benefits. To start, identify the goals for your content, the intended audience, and topics that might appeal to that audience. Discover where your readers live online and find out which sites and social channels they use to find similar content and news.

Increasingly, this research is something that can be automated, and even quantified, through social analytics platforms. After you've identified possibilities, focus on one or two target media channels. This could be an online magazine, trade publication, business periodical, podcast, blog, or traditional media outlet. Study these channels. Learn about the editorial policies. Immerse yourself in the content forms used by the sites. Set a goal of creating one superb and relevant piece of content for that channel. Each quarter, turn to another new channel and repeat the process.

2. Establish a distribution process.

Your organization should be constantly researching potential new distribution sites and assessing all content for distribution potential. One large company I work with reviews every piece of content they produce and determines at least three other ways it can be used. They might pitch a publication, turn it into a SlideShare presentation, or suggest it as an interview topic with a favorite podcaster. Are you putting your content through a similar distribution gate?

3. Consider an organizational shift focused on distribution.

Some companies are beginning to take "brand journalism" very seriously. The old idea of a company copywriter is being transformed into a full-blown media creation department. Some companies are exploring content development newsrooms for external sourcing as well as traditional marketing communications functions.

4. Explore the idea of employee networks.

Establishing a "social organization" is a long-term aspirational goal for many companies, but there's no reason you can't ask enthusiastic employees to help spread interesting, relevant content on their social networks. The amplification effect can be significant—much greater than traditional distribution through the logo-infused company sites.

If you have 20 interested employees, that's 20 potential networks you can tap into if they're willing to volunteer to help. Many employees are enthusiastic about the idea of igniting content from their employer and becoming involved in the marketing process. Some companies also tap suppliers and business partners to share their content, which they're normally happy to do.

5. Don't overlook email as a distribution channel for your content.

For many people, email is still the preferred method of communicating and sharing information. Are you making people aware of your content through regular emails? You are sending regular emails, aren't you? Remember that email subscribers may be the closest thing you have to a record of your Alpha Audience. These are the people who have raised their hands and said, "Market to me!" Let them know of new opportunities to consume and share your content.

6. Discover and master new platforms.

Every company is pouring content into blogs, Facebook, Twitter, and YouTube. But there are literally hundreds of other viable and popular platforms to explore as less-crowded niche distribution options. Here are a few you might be overlooking:

- **Quora:** Founded by ex-Facebook executives, this site is determined to answer every question. Conduct a site search for topics relevant to your business and you're certain to find questions to weigh-in on.
- **LinkedIn:** Of course LinkedIn is familiar as a business networking site, but it's also one of the largest business publishing sites in the world. It's an excellent place to distribute existing content, especially if you're B2B.
- **StumbleUpon:** The unique value proposition of this site is its randomness. People "stumble" for content submitted by users. If people upvote and like the content, it's more likely to show up in the random streams. If content gets "hot" on StumbleUpon, it can ignite very quickly!
- **Pinterest:** Many content creators claim there's no better way to ignite content than through a "pin" on Pinterest. All you need is an attractive graphic that links back to your original content. Even industrial companies like General Electric have been using this strategy to connect to new audiences.
- **Quibb:** This network emerged in 2013 as a promising platform to share content into specific industry verticals.
- **Reddit:** Reddit is an enormous content community boasting more than 100 million unique monthly visitors. The platform's key innovation is its voting system. Anything there—pictures, questions, comments—can be "upvoted" or "downvoted" by its users. Stuff that gets the most positive votes gets

moved to the top of the "best posts" or list of comments. Hitting the front page of the "best posts" list creates a loop where its prominence on the site earns more votes ... and virality. Reddit is a home to passionate people who are willing to spend 20–30 minutes researching and writing a reply in return for a mere thank you. But tread carefully: There are very strict rules about promotional content! Reddit can also be a very rich source of content ideas.

7. Consider micro sites.

When researching possible new distribution channels, don't just look at the large, noisy places. Sometimes finding a niche channel with only 50 subscribers can be a goldmine, if they're the right 50 people who could become Alpha Audience fanatics.

For example, one management consultant in Philadelphia is tapping into small professional LinkedIn Groups like "Philadelphia Accountants" and "Philly HR Professionals" to connect his content to relevant people in his sales area. If more than a few people are interested in your niche, chances are there's an online community out there dedicated to it. When you find these communities, don't just spam your article and leave. Engage with people and build a reputation as an authority within your space that will attract new Alphas.

8. Form content partnerships.

If your content pipeline is constrained, consider partnering with another pipeline. This technique is commonly called *brandscaping*. For example, the insurance company Geico ran a series of commercials featuring icons from other companies, like the Pillsbury Doughboy. This strategy makes Geico appealing to Pillsbury fans as well as its own.

9. Look for opportunities for newsjacking.

A term coined by David Meerman Scott, *newsjacking* describes a process to align your brand message with breaking news events so you ride a wave of traditional media coverage. A few years ago, when the Catholic Church was about to name a new pope, Notre Dame University informed all the major news outlets that it would have expert commentators standing by when the news broke. When white smoke emerged from the Sistine Chapel, the Notre Dame experts showed up on every major new channel.

Real time marketing can drive conversions and sales, says Scott. When MultiCare Health System[1] identified a trending topic, eclampsia, during an emotional episode of the hit TV series *"Downton Abbey,"* the healthcare network published a blog post about the condition within hours of the episode's airdate. MultiCare Health saw over 1,000 page views, with people spending an average of five minutes on the page. They also received 30 click-throughs to their online appointment system.

10. Use Facebook as a distribution channel.

It's popular to bash Facebook but the channel's inevitable world dominance also means it's a marketing channel you can't ignore. Despite the premature predictions of the channel's demise, it continues to be a wildly popular social network across many demographics throughout most of the world. One study showed that 74 percent of all marketers name Facebook as the most important channel for their content distribution.[2]

For many companies, Facebook is the most cost effective way for brands to distribute content at scale. Of course a lot depends on the nature of your content, message, and core audience, but don't overlook Facebook as a method of content distribution.

11. Crowdsource content creation and distribution.

Involving experts in your content usually assures access to their networks, too. This accounts for the popularity of round-up posts from well-known authors and experts. Even including one quote from an expert, or a reference to one of their blog posts or books, can ignite your content. If you highlight them in the content, they're likely to help you promote the piece too.

12. Syndicate.

Almost every industry has some resource that's curating relevant, timely content and summarizing it in a regular newsletter, website, or newsfeed. If a curated content site doesn't exist in your niche, consider starting one. It's a helpful way to keep industry leaders on top of the news, and it can position your company as the go-to place for valuable information.

If curation services already exist, develop relationships with these resources and learn what it takes to add your content in the channel. In addition to the obvious exposure, this work can also lead new audience members to your home site and possibly provide valuable backlinks that will enhance your status with search engines.

I want to conclude this section with some sage advice from journalist Dorie Clark. Dorie has built her brand almost entirely through other people's distribution channels, including

Forbes and *Harvard Business Review.* But it's not a perfect strategy, and it requires balance. There's a risk supplying content to platforms that you don't own.

"I go back and forth about this distribution strategy," she said. "On one hand, you can get an immediate boost of credibility from associating with well-known brands, and when you're first starting out, you really need that. You also have access to an established readership base that otherwise might not discover you.

"But the downside is that *Forbes* or the *Harvard Business Review* owns those readers and those relationships, not you. It's a much slower, but perhaps more valuable, process to build readership on your own blog or content site. I've tried to thread the needle by continuing to blog for larger outlets but try to drive people (through my bio links or by mentioning my site in the body of the article) to my website, where they'll hopefully sign up for my mailing list. Growing my mailing list substantially is one of my top goals going forward, because it's so critical to be able to speak directly to my readers."

Advertising and Paid Media

In a podcast discussion, the always thought-provoking Mitch Joel said to me: "I wonder if in the near future, paid advertising will be the only way we can ignite our content."

Certainly that's a strong statement and a sentiment expressed by many frustrated marketers. In any event, a paid promotional strategy integrated with other content tactics has become a staple of most digital marketing efforts.

Organic reach is based on the assumption that you have to earn your way into the newsfeed with great content that people love. Paying to increase your exposure can dramatically increase the impact and engagement of each piece of content, and it can be relatively cost effective, especially considering the time required to work through other content distribution efforts. The paid option also usually comes with analytics to help you measure the effectiveness of your effort and optimize into the future.

Here's a summary of paid distribution options that might be a part of an overall content ignition strategy:

Advertising networks

Popular options include Google AdWords, Facebook and Twitter ads, Outbrain, and OneSpot. There are many strategies for using advertising networks, but they're especially effective when you need to ramp up initial awareness at the beginning of a campaign, when you don't have time to build an audience, or when the issue and content is particularly time sensitive (like an event). The primary formats for digital ads are:

- **Pay per click (PPC)**: The most common paid method. When a user clicks on the ad, the marketer pays for each click.
- **Search PPC**: Requires the marketer to identify specific keywords. When searched by a potential customer, the ad will display on the page of search results.
- **Content PPC**: Appears as content suggestions on sites, often underneath similar articles.

Retargeted advertising

Keeps track of people who visit your site and displays your ads to them as they visit other sites online. Technically all that is necessary is a JavaScript tag in the footer of your website. This code creates a list of people who visit your site by placing anonymous retargeting cookies in their browser. This list allows retargeting vendors to display ads to your potential customers as they visit other sites. It's relatively straightforward to set up, and it's a demonstration of how paid media reinforces great content by intelligently distributing it with discretion.

Sponsored content

Facebook, Twitter, LinkedIn, and many other platforms offer paid opportunities to selectively boost the visibility of your content. The advantage is that you increase awareness to your current audience as well as others in a very precise demographic category. Sponsored content is a good way to increase exposure to highly targeted audiences and possibly attract new viewers for your content.

Native advertising

The Interactive Advertising Bureau defines *native advertising* as "paid ads that are so cohesive with the page content, assimilated into the design, and consistent with the platform behavior that the viewer simply feels that they belong." According to the IAB, native advertising contains six different types of ad units: in-feed, promoted listings, in-ad with native element, paid search, recommendation widgets, and custom.

By partnering with publishers, your content is integrated into the interface of a media company's site. One example is the paid editorial features on the *Forbes* website. Native advertising provides the credibility of being associated with the media brand, validation of being featured in the editorial portion of a site, and opportunity for vast exposure to a relevant audience.

However, it's also a controversial strategy as traditional publishers devote increasing space to "advertorials" that at times can be indistinguishable from the publisher's content. Sponsored articles have received pushback from some publishers, brands, consumers, and even government regulators who are concerned because the articles resemble editorial content. One commenter described it this way: "How about we try treating our audience with a little more respect and intelligence? Native advertising is the uninvited guest who makes his predicament worse through a seeming lack of self-awareness and clumsy attempts to fit in."

This misdirection can damage the editorial integrity of a publication, as well as a brand's image. The only way this strategy works in the long-term is by focusing on providing relevant content that equals the quality of the content in the editorial portion of the site.

Social media advertising

In addition to boosting stories, most of the major social media sites offer paid opportunities to attract new audience members, own a trending topic, and access specific people outside your network. Some social media platforms with vast audiences like Reddit and StumbleUpon let you buy clicks to your content at very low prices from socially-engaged visitors.

Chad Pollitt is the cofounder of an online magazine called *Relevance* devoted to studying content promotion techniques. Here are some of his "native social" best practices:

- **Brands that use paid social media must remember it's a marketplace.** How they target interests, connections, behavior, demographics, and geography all impact the cost of a campaign. Facebook in particular has over a million interests that can be targeted and Twitter has even more. As a result, targeting many long-tail interests that might be considered sub-interests of a broader category can help brands cut campaign costs by as much as 90 percent.

- **Marketers have to establish measurable goals for the content they wish to promote on paid social channels because they dictate which channels to use and how to allocate budget.** For example, distributing content (like a blog post) at scale every time new content is published is probably cost prohibitive. However, marketers wishing to promote a sweepstakes, webinar, or eBook may find promoting on social channels well worth the cost.

- **After goals are established, marketers should track each channel's performance by cost per click, cost per action, or cost per lead.** Although the analytics provided by social networks continue to increase in sophistication, it's probable that you will need a combination of these outside metrics and inside metrics to determine the cost/benefit of each channel.

- Marketers should never equate the click in "cost per click" with a visitor to a website. A click in social media can equate to a like, share, profile view, comment, favorite, etc. Actual website traffic for every click that is paid for can be as little as one-sixteenth of the total actions gained by the campaign.

Promotion

When I think of promoting content on the web, I imagine a circus performer walking on a high wire between two skyscrapers. Without a net. Blindfolded. A daredevil act like that depends on an enormous amount of experience, judgment, and balance to stay one misstep away from ruin.

When promoting content, there's a thin line between being helpful and being obnoxious. For decades, marketers have been conditioned to shout and broadcast, and it just seems natural to turn to the new social channels to do the same thing! But blasting promotions to that precious Alpha Audience isn't winning you new friends—it's spamming.

As a wise marketer, you should use social media to network with peers, colleagues, and your strongest supporters to *let others tell your story* to every extent possible.

Here are 10 practical tips to promote your content without crossing the spam line.

1. Look for questions to answer.

Have you considered using your blog posts to help people solve problems? It's a subtle but clever promotion technique. There are thousands of people asking questions on LinkedIn Groups, Quora, and sites like Yahoo Answers. Find questions you can answer, then add a link to one of your helpful posts as a response. This type of promotion accomplishes three things:

- You leverage your content in a truly helpful way.
- You attract a relevant new audience and drive them to your content.
- You extend the value of your content because these forum answers have a long shelf life.

2. Using the social channels.

Your audience spends time on social media to play Farmville, view photos of Grumpy Cat, and complain about the government. They don't want to be marketed to, sold to, or advertised to. However, if you've attracted a loyal audience who's interested in you and your business, they're probably interested in some of your business-related content too. Not necessarily all the time, not even every day perhaps, but it is perfectly fine to pepper your social media posts with relevant business news every now and then. There is no hard and fast rule for this—if you get too spammy, you'll probably hear about it!

3. Include content links in your Google profile.

While you're busy creating content in various formats, it's easy to forget that your Google profile is the perfect container for links to all that content and serves as your business card for many people looking for you on the web. If you haven't updated your profile in a while, go check it out. (I'll wait right here for you.)

Data scientist Christopher Penn of SHIFT Communications explains, "It's also absolutely essential to use Google's Structured Data software to identify your site. This is what controls Google's display of your information in search results. It's arcane, but huge and important." Do a search for "Google Structured Data" to find Google's tool to test your site to see if there are any obvious errors keeping Google from finding and properly displaying your content.

4. Link to content on other social media profiles.

LinkedIn lets you insert media links in your profile, and the summary and project sections are ideal for featuring your content. LinkedIn also owns SlideShare and can display thumbnails of your presentations as well as highlights of your blog content. On Facebook, highlight your podcast, blog, and other content in your profile. My Twitter profile contains a link to a landing page where people can find all of my content properties.

5. Make the most of unused real estate on business cards and other business properties.

If you have several content properties like I do, trying to list them on a business card can be a challenge. That's why I have links to all my sites on the *back* of my card. I've created short, easy to remember links through bit.ly. For example, the link to my blog on my business card is bit.ly/grow-blog, which is much easier to list and remember than http://www.businessesgrow.com/blog. You can watch your links on bit.ly to see who is clicking through and sharing your content.

Be sure to list ways to access your content below your email signature. Some people even promote their latest blog post or video in that space.

6. Ignite snippets.

Every post you write probably has a few short quotable gems that people might like to share (because it makes them look cooler, smarter, funnier, etc!). There are several plug-ins that allow people to tweet specific quotes right from the text of your post. You also can embed short quotes on slides in your live presentations. By spoon-feeding content in this fashion, you make it easy for people to ignite your ideas right from their seats in the meeting or conference room.

7. Participate in link roundups.

Many bloggers curate their favorite blog posts into daily, weekly, or monthly link roundups. You can find link roundups in your market by searching for keywords like "link roundup" or "weekly link roundup." If you want to find blogs that are specifically related to your market, add a modifier like "link roundup" + marketing or "link roundup" + parenting. Contact the blog owner and send them a link to your latest blog post. If you use this technique judiciously and send bloggers only your very best content, there's a good chance they will eventually link to you.

8. Promote new content within old content.

Here's a little trick to introduce blog readers to new content. Use a tool like Social Crawlytics to determine your most-shared content over the last few years. Chances are your best work is still attracting new readers. After you've identified the most trafficked and shared pages on your site, add links to relevant keywords that point to your new content. Another trick is to embed your own ads on these popular posts to promote services and other content. For example, on my most popular Twitter-related posts (which still get hundreds of views each year) I have a graphic at the end promoting my book *The Tao of Twitter*.

9. Join a content-sharing club.

There are a number of sites where you can join other content creators to share and support each other's efforts. One popular site is Triberr, which is like a blogging club where you can discover and share content in a reciprocal fashion. This interaction provides an opportunity for entirely new audiences to discover your content.

10. Send a personalized note or email to bloggers in your industry.

Adding a personal touch to your promotion strategies can provide powerful results. If you have a valuable piece of content you want shared around the blogosphere, find bloggers who have written similar content, compliment them on their work, and suggest that they might enjoy the post you've written on the similar topic. In the blogging world, "enjoy" is a euphemism for "share!" Some resources to help you locate bloggers with relevant content are:

- Topsy.com
- BuzzSumo.com
- Alltop.com
- Twellow.com
- CircleCount.com

Create a personalized subject line and carefully craft the email so it doesn't come across as a form letter. If you make any mistakes in the email (like calling them by the wrong name!) it's likely that you have ruined all chances for further connection. Point out a specific connection between the blogger and the content you're bringing to their attention. Did you link to their post? That's a big hook.

Search Engine Optimization

I'm constantly amazed that the world has created a $30 billion industry designed to trick Google. Okay, okay, there's more to SEO than that. And every marketing plan certainly needs to consider optimizing for search because your work can't ignite if it can't be found.

There are tons of blogs and video sites devoted to the cult of optimizing content for search. An extensive tutorial is beyond the scope of this book—and unnecessary because there is simply so much free content out there for you to enjoy.

Instead, it's more useful to limit our coverage of this complex subject to the topic of ignition and three questions: 1) Does SEO ignite content?; 2) Does social sharing affect SEO?; 3) What do you need to know about SEO to be effective in moving your content?

Does SEO ignite content?

Without question, considering SEO is essential to getting your content discovered. Of course, like anything, it's a matter of degree and the priority *type* for investment in SEO will vary enormously by industry and by your objectives. I suggest that setting priorities for SEO might vary by content as well.

Let's connect some dots between viral, SEO, and content type through a case study. Take a look at this chart that shows traffic to my blog over the course of a year:

BLOG TRAFFIC PEAKS

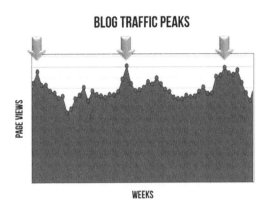

As you can see, there were three posts that drove extraordinary traffic to my website in this year. These are the posts:

- January: "Content Shock," introducing an idea of economic evaluation of content[3]
- June: "70 Rising Stars of Social Media," highlighting lesser-known marketing talents[4]
- November: "A Speech You Will Never Hear Again," revealing how personal pain had a silver lining[5]

These posts would be considered *hero content* based on my definition in Chapter 2. To review, this pattern companies use to build a brand over time requires three types of content:

- **Hygiene content**, which takes care of everyday customer needs and is the most likely target for search engine traffic.
- **Hub content**, which tells a deeper story and connects people to your brand.
- **Hero content**, which creates broad awareness through viral distribution.

Of these, hero content is by far the most difficult to produce. You just can't plan for viral. And yet each of my three "viral" posts did have common qualities that transcended the ordinary daily drumming of the web.

1. Their popularity had nothing to do with SEO.

Ironically, these three posts were my least-search-optimized posts of the year. I mean, what kind of search traffic does "content shock" drive? It was a made-up term!

Isn't this an interesting idea? We're supposed to pay attention to SEO to drive blog traffic, and yet premeditated SEO played absolutely no role in these three successes. Why?

When I wrote these posts I mindfully tossed SEO aside and wrote great content that I knew people would love. Think about it this way: If you're stuffing your content with popular search terms, how original—how heroic—can it possibly be? By definition, competing for SEO terms forces you to out-duel somebody else for keyword supremacy. Creating content with a chance to go viral forces you to stand in a place where you create an entirely new keyword—and supremacy based on originality. And Google seems to love that.

2. The content was long.

These three posts were not only popular, but they were also *the three longest posts I wrote all year.* Sort of validates the research covered in the shareability chapter, right? Longer posts sometimes have a better chance for massive social sharing.

3. The content was distinctive.

Great marketing begins with great content. These pieces were unique and conversational. In all three cases, nothing had ever been written like these posts. I took personal risks with this content, too—taking a stand, trying a new format, providing intense personal disclosure.

As this case study suggests, whether or not you emphasize SEO depends on the specific goal for your content. SEO isn't a universal solution for content ignition; rather, it's dependent on the *type* of content you're producing. This graphic summarizes the relationship between content ignition and SEO:

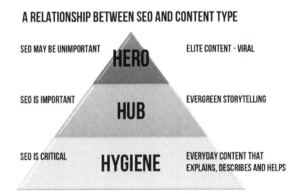

A RELATIONSHIP BETWEEN SEO AND CONTENT TYPE

SEO MAY BE UNIMPORTANT — **HERO** — ELITE CONTENT - VIRAL

SEO IS IMPORTANT — **HUB** — EVERGREEN STORYTELLING

SEO IS CRITICAL — **HYGIENE** — EVERYDAY CONTENT THAT EXPLAINS, DESCRIBES AND HELPS

This theory suggests that for most content, SEO is an essential part of the discovery process. On the other hand, being wedded to SEO best practices (popular keywords in headlines, links, and copy) may actually inhibit the ability for content to attain massive reach.

A grand irony: My Content Shock article, written with no SEO in mind, produced hundreds of valuable backlinks from many of the most respected blogs in the business. By ignoring SEO, I had my biggest SEO success in the history of the blog.

And that is a nice lead-in to the second big question about SEO ...

Does social transmission ignite SEO?

There is no single tactic or magic trick that will blast you to the top of the search rankings. Instead, achieving good search engine performance requires strategically leveraging three key areas—links, content, and promotion. Each of these areas works together to create a successful SEO strategy.

While there is general agreement about these strategic foundations, there is enormous debate about how social signals like tweets and Likes figure into Google's top-secret search algorithm. It stands to reason that a piece of content tweeted 25,000 times might be more meaningful to consumers than something tweeted twice, right?

Not so fast. Google has repeatedly denied that it's using social signals for SEO ranking purposes, although some studies do show correlations between social sharing and search performance. But the debate is irrelevant because there surely is a sharing benefit to search.

The days of competitive link building, the hallmark of SEO best practices for years, is over. Google doesn't want anyone building links through wacky schemes. But they do want people creating extremely relevant content that the company can serve to its search customers (and eventually monetize through ads). So Google is looking for signals that we're earning those valuable links. Of course great content can't *assure* links ... but if you could ignite that content, it just might tip the odds a little bit in your favor by getting your work in the hands of more people who can link to you naturally.

An example of this idea in action is the very creative content ignition strategy pioneered by Lee Odden of TopRank Marketing. To promote various marketing conference clients, his team has created a series of eBooks featuring ideas from well-known speakers presented in creative themes like detectives, rock-n-roll, and Alice in Wonderland. If Odden tried to rank against very crowded terms like "content marketing secrets," his content would never be found. But by igniting the content through paid, earned, and owned media strategies, people hear about the content and begin searching for something like "content wonderland." In essence, awareness through content sharing is creating a built-in SEO benefit.

"I know that's not what a buyer would normally search on, but when you see the buzz about the e books we've created, a lot of people will become interested in those ideas and then they will validate them by searching on them," Odden said.

"We're literally creating our own unique search demand with projects like this, and believe me, something that seems silly like Content Wonderland will become searched on a heck of a lot with just a few weeks of promotion. Of course, we're optimizing any assets that are being created for anticipated search terms. But, we're also looking to create demand by getting people to talk about and share what we have produced. We want to generate buzz."

So although Google states that tweets and Facebook Likes don't directly affect search results, there is an indirect connection if those actions somehow lead to a new audience connecting with legitimately great content and valuable backlinks result.

What do you need to know about SEO to be effective in moving your content?

For the third and final SEO-related question, let's turn again to Lee Odden, author of *Optimize*, a leading book on this concept.

A short time ago, optimizing content for search was fairly straightforward. There were checklists with standardized tasks to help Google find you. But the field is far more complicated today. How should you approach this, even if you don't have a large budget for link-building strategies?

"I do think there are still categories of standard activities that persist," Odden says, "but the SEO checklists are quite different and fairly limited. I think of SEO as marketing performance optimization relative to search, advertising, email, content … anything you're using to build your business.

"You're collecting data. You're collecting key performance indicators as evidence that you're on the right track toward your goals, and you use those data-based insights to course correct and optimize the performance of your content strategy.

"With SEO, of course, there are still traditional things one can do to help Google do its job because Google is far from perfect! Google has made some choices that have drastically affected websites that had relied heavily on organic search as the source of new business. Those businesses had to make substantial changes, especially when it comes to links and link sources. Many of the link-building strategies have been killed off by Google. Companies used to pay an SEO to get the most links. Now, they're paying those SEOs to remove those links.

"There are things we can do technically and from a content alignment perspective that make it easier for Google to understand who we are, what we stand for, and whether we're the best choice for the thing that somebody is searching for.

"SEO today is much more focused on content and relationships. We will always need keyword strategies and research but first and foremost, content moves because we're creating something cool that people will *want* to see and share. Everything starts with the quality of the content. We need to make it easy for people who are involved in the content to share. The content has to make them feel something and make them proud to share it because they love to share it, not because somebody is asking them.

"Obviously, we're going to promote the content. We look for ways to repurpose content. For the conference we worked with, we had an infographic that was created from e-books. We had tweetable quotes in this infographic. We had graphical illustrations of great influencer quotes as another piece of quality content that was easy to share. We made Twitter lists of the speakers and profiles of the speakers which will be brought into Pinterest and other things that deconstruct the eBook content. We published interviews with the speakers as additional promotion. The day the eBook went live, we provided tweets and embed codes for the slide deck to the participants as well as our broader network.

"I also think influencer outreach is part of the SEO formula these days. I've been publishing all kinds of things for many years. Every time I do this I expand the number of people who I have worked with, and I can go back and say, 'Hey, you remember this thing we did. I've got another one coming out. If you care to take a look at and share it, great, if you don't, that's cool too.'"

We'll continue these insights from Lee in Chapter 10. You see, we'll need him to help us unravel the final element of the Content Code, the highly mysterious subject of Authority. But first let's cover one of my favorite marketing subjects, social proof. It's time for a quiz. Are you ready?

CHAPTER NINE

Social Signals and Social Proof

"Sincerity – if you can fake that, you've got it made."
– George Burns

'd like to do a test on you—right here, right now. Ready?

Imagine that you move to a new home with a lovely yard and you're interested in starting a rose garden. Roses can be tricky plants to grow, so you need information to help guide you through the best practices for a beginning gardener. Like most people, you start with a web search, and you're delighted to find that the top two search results fit your needs precisely. Both articles are brimming with tips, detailed guides, and illustrations to get you going. One of these articles has been tweeted five times. The other one has been tweeted 452 times.

Which one will you read?

I've used this little test in hundreds of classes before thousands of students and not one person—not one!—has ever answered that they would read the post with five tweets.

My friend, you have just experienced the awesome power of social proof! All things being equal, in a case like this the quality of the content doesn't really matter. Neither does the heroic brand of the author, the credibility of the publication, the distribution, promotion, or clever SEO. The content is poised to ignite simply because of a number.

Putting social proof to work

We use social proof as a shortcut in our real-world decision-making every day. Things seem easier to buy when others validate that it's a smart option.

Social proof is powerful in situations where people don't have the facts they need to make an informed decision. To help resolve uncertainty, people look for clues in their environment to help them determine their best guess at "truth." They assume the actions of others reflect the correct behavior for them, too. Just as the number of tweets on the gardening post influenced your decision of what to read, behavior is driven by the assumption that people in the same situation may possess more knowledge about what is correct, popular, or ideal. For example:

- "Look at all the awards and plaques on that person's wall! She must be really smart. I feel good about being here."

- "Everybody in this room has an Apple computer. It must be a great computer."
- "There's a long line of people waiting to get into that bar. We should probably go there, too, since we don't know the city very well."

Social proof is so powerful that after repeated exposures, people even begin to internalize an acceptance of the belief as truth because so many others *must* be correct.

Social proof is an especially critical concept to understand in an online world of overwhelming information density. With so much content available, we're starved for clues to help us know who to trust, what to believe, and what company can help us as quickly as possible. So we tend to follow the numbers, especially if the decision is low-risk. We normally don't cross-reference information or check sources. We look for the biggest number and believe in its authority.

Social proof is also a more important factor of influence online versus offline because our choices are public. We may not care much about something we buy for our homes if nobody sees it, but with the whole world watching on the Internet, we very much care about how we appear, what we choose, and what we disclose to others.

Social proof and online ignition

In the offline world, people don't walk around with their number of Facebook "Likes" plastered on their foreheads, but in the world of social media, numerical proxies for authority abound like fleas on a shaggy mutt. For example, blogs that generate a lot of tweets and comments may get to a point where they're popular just because they're popular, while worthy blogs may never get noticed unless they receive a boost in validation through social proof. On the web, entire business models may be built on social proof, giving them earned or unearned authority.

"In the online world, social proof is what makes you legitimate," said Jay Baer.[1] "There are small cues on the web that convey this type of authority. There's a very good reason bloggers keep a tweet counter open at the top of their sites. If a post has been tweeted 100 times, the assumption is that it's worthy of your attention. Well, truthfully, maybe it is, maybe it isn't. There are different ways to game the on-line system and still be recognized as an authority. It's much easier to create a scenario and be seen as an authority online than it is to become a truly authoritative person off-line."

At no other time in history has the appearance of authority been so easily assumed and promoted. Words like "bestselling," "award-winning," and "expert" have been rendered almost meaningless. People crave any possible shortcut to rapidly distill meaning from the information-overloaded world. Unfortunately, in this setting, the badges of influence may become even more important than legitimate authority built from true knowledge and experience!

"How much do you think we'd be talking about Twitter followers or Facebook Likes if the number wasn't attached to your public profile?" said Baer. "We care about Twitter followers and Facebook Likes disproportionately not because of the power of the medium, but because we keep score in public. Every legitimate social media consultant will tell you that it's not about how many Twitter followers or Facebook Likes you have, it's what you do with them. And in terms of driving measurable behavior, conversions, revenue, loyalty, and advocacy, they are of course correct. Number of Twitter followers doesn't mean a thing, right? Wrong. The reality is that social media measurement is a very public competition, and we buy it hook, line, and sinker. Why would politicians not only (allegedly) pay to build a following that dwarfs the other candidates, but then have the audacity/stupidity to brag about the advantage? Because it matters in the court of public perception.

"We may not like it. We may not even choose to admit it. But it's disingenuous to suggest that number of Twitter followers has no impact on how you or your organizations are viewed by the vox populi. It's not a key performance indicator, it's a key popularity indicator."

It's unsettling to think that the local blogger with the fake Twitter followers or a blog site with manufactured social proof may very well accrue benefits of influence in an unequal measure to the actual skills and talents of their creators. Scarcity of time and the pressures of daily life make people default to interacting with those few who matter—or at least who *appear* to matter—and reciprocate their attention. *The implication is that a possible marker of authority like Likes and followers can make an impact on people and contribute to the perception of your status and influence. Even if it's dead wrong.*

While this may seem outrageous, as business professionals we have to deal with what is, not what we would like it to be, and the fact that the world is full of pretenders is nothing new—it's just that these days they may have an opportunity to find innocent victims on the Internet on a much grander scale while eluding reprisal with the simple push of a computer key.

The care and nurturing of these badges of social proof is big business and an important source of perceived influence. In the long term, people will probably make decisions about your true influence based on your opinions and content. But in the short term, badges are an important part of social proof and a factor of content transmission.

Strategies for social proof

Strong social proof makes you more confident that you're in the right place and the content before you is share-worthy. Weak social proof is like walking into a restaurant at 7 p.m. and being the only customers there. It's a bit unnerving and lonely, and you might wonder if you should turn around and leave. But if the restaurant is filled and lively—perhaps there is even a wait for a table—you feel better about being there. Social proof works the same way. Symbols of traction make you want to be involved and buy in, whether it's a restaurant, an online video, or a Pinterest page.

To help your content really take off, it has to take off a little bit first. Here's an example of what I mean. A Fortune 100 company (whom I will not identify!) is putting a tremendous amount of effort into its blog. In fact, 90 different people are active bloggers for this company. The content is well-written, interesting, relevant, and timely. But despite the fact that this company has more than 300,000 employees, the average number of social shares for a typical blog post is five. The message that number sends? "Even we don't care."

If this company were to ask only a portion of the 90 people involved in writing the blog to also ignite it on Twitter, LinkedIn, and Facebook, it would certainly improve the probability that more organic sharing would be coming its way.

My sincere hope is that you will never cheat your way into favorable social proof. If you're trying to build a lasting brand and a meaningful Alpha Audience, radical honesty is the only way to build trust. Character equates to power in the long run. Here are 10 ethical ways to "prime the pump" on social proof and improve the perceived credibility of your content:

- **Promote your content "As seen on …":** Have you been quoted or featured on a well-known blog, newspaper, or television show? Don't keep it a secret. Many content creators use "As seen on …" testimonies to display where they have appeared, powerful social proof.
- **Request endorsements:** Here's the cool thing about LinkedIn endorsements—they're public and permanent. And you can use them anywhere. Go ahead and ask some of your favorite customers for a recommendation and then promote the heck out of them.
- **Take advantage of friends and family:** If you're just starting a content-creation effort, don't be shy about asking for help. Explain to everyone you know how important it is to get your blog off the ground and ask them for a little Twitter or Facebook love. Ask them to leave a comment, too, while they're at it!
- **Activate employees:** Every person in your company has a stake in making your marketing as successful as possible. Identify employees who are social media enthusiasts and ask them to help support the effort with some social sharing. Devoted employees usually feel proud about participating in marketing activities.

You may even send out an email once a week with suggested tweets that they can either post as written or use as inspiration.

- **Highlight testimonials:** Dr. Gary Schirr of Radford University left this review of my book *Social Media Explained*: "Mark Schaefer is the master of great little books about marketing." That's a great validation, so I have that quote posted on several sites featuring my book, including Amazon. If your company collects testimonials, sprinkle them throughout your website on the pages you know will be seen often. A quote from someone who says she learned valuable lessons from your content can help persuade a visitor who's not sure whether or not to subscribe to your content channel.

- **Promote badges:** Visit any university website and I guarantee you'll find at least one badge on the site touting something like "Named one of the Top 10 Business Schools in Southeast New Mexico." Everyone is known for something. If you're listed, named, featured, or honored ... let people know.

- **Focus on powerful customer reviews:** When is the last time you made a meaningful purchase on Amazon or an eCommerce site without glancing at the reviews? Scoring systems are powerful social proof, but don't get too upset about a few negative reviews. Nobody's perfect, and the balance actually adds to the credibility of the reviews.

- **Keep track of subscriber counts:** People feel comfortable joining the crowd. Many sites feature a counter with numbers of subscribers to a content channel. Hubspot has a simple call to action on their site: "Subscribe to our blog. Thousands of others have."

- **Collect kudos tweets:** When people tweet nice things about you, start saving them as a "favorite" tweet. Then you can link to the list of nice recommendations as an entire stream of public, published social validation, as in "Don't take my word for it, click here to see what others are saying about my (book, blog, podcast …)."

- **Publicize clients:** *Logo porn* is a popular website tactic of displaying client logos. It's an easy way to establish credibility for your company by simply showing who you work with. Some companies (especially large ones) require permission before you can post a logo on your site. I've added this as a contract line item: "Schaefer Marketing Solutions may name you as a client on its website." Customers are usually happy to help you out in this way.

When social proof backfires

I need to end this tidy little chapter with a cautionary note. A few years ago, I made a business decision to remove nearly all social proof from my website. In essence, I'm not following my own advice. Here's my story.

In the early days of blogging, there was a metric sponsored by *Advertising Age* magazine called the Power 150, a listing of the most powerful marketing blogs on earth. It was not even close to being a reliable metric. Part of it was determined by some dude who decided if he liked how your blog looked. No joke. The "Todd Score." I actually increased my score by writing Todd an email asking him to give me an extra point. Twice. Some of the blogs on the list had been inactive for two years. It was that bad.

But like many bloggers of the day, I became obsessed with this social proof. I put a badge on my site that displayed my daily score for all the world to see. The {grow} blog was number 37 or 22 or whatever "Todd" had decided, I suppose. I would flip out when it dropped. Instead of focusing on great content, I started concentrating on pulling any string that would increase my score for a couple days. And it was a metric that really proved nothing. I also had seven or eight other badges on my site from every meaningless "best of" list I was on—arbitrary awards created largely to boost egos. Social proof became a distraction, a sickness really.

Finally my head won out over my ego and I knew I had to do a purge. My personal philosophy had always been "create great content, love on your audience, and the rest will take care of itself." I had lost my way. In 10 minutes, I had ripped down every badge, every brag, and every testimony on the blog—I stripped it down to words on a page.

Immediately I was reenergized and refocused on surprising and delighting my readers with every post. Removing the distraction of badges and awards helped me work on what was going to move the needle in the end—building an engaged Alpha Audience through insanely great content and my undivided attention. Soon, I didn't have any idea where I ranked on any list, and I've never looked back!

This is not to judge anyone else who uses social proof as a marketing technique. I just wrote an entire chapter advocating it! It's smart business and an undeniably important piece of the

Content Code. It just didn't work for my personality so beware if you start watching those numbers too often!

You're closing in on the end of the book now. Let's take a look at one final and subtle factor that ignites content … and it has very little to do with content!

CHAPTER TEN

The Mystery of Authority

*"We know that no one ever seizes power with the intention
of relinquishing it." – George Orwell*

Congratulations! You've made it to the final of the six
elements of the Content Code, and it's all about *authority*, an element cloaked in secrecy and mystery.

If I were to depict the "BADASS" model faithfully,
it would actually look like this: BADaSS. You see,
compared to the gargantuan stature of our first five subjects,
this one is … well … tiny by comparison. Authority is the one
element of content ignition that is most out of your control, at
least in the short-term. Although elusive, it's also a factor of
great importance because if you can attain the power of site
authority, you also achieve a near-permanent advantage for
content ignition.

Let me explain the importance of site (or domain) authority with a sad little tale.

One of the seeds for this book was the Content Shock blog post I mentioned all the way back in Chapter 2. This post had all the elements of great, shareable content, and it really ignited with my Alpha Audience … and beyond! The post was shared thousands of time and attracted hundreds of comments. Talk about social proof! In just a short time, dozens of other content pieces had been created all over the web, linking back to my idea and my post.

A week after the article ran, I did a Google search for the term "Content Shock" to see what others might have written about my commentary. To my utter amazement, my own post—the original idea—came up THIRD in the rankings … on a search term I had just *made up* a few days before!

This seems impossible, doesn't it? The reason this alternative content leaped over my own original post was due to something called *Domain Authority* (also known as *site authority or site rank*). The fact that the other two sites were bigger and more well-known in the eyes of Google than my own little website gave them a critical, and somewhat permanent, edge in the search rankings.

The most important content did not rise to the top. The most important websites did.

The "let's figure out Google" cottage industry of experts estimates that a rating of the trustworthiness and authority of a website accounts for nearly 25 percent of the overall search ranking algorithm. There's a tight connection between Google's site rank and the public search results used to discover your content. No wonder my post lost out when it was stacked against mega-blogs with hundreds of thousands of readers!

SEO and digital relationships

Lee Odden, the CEO of TopRank Marketing and a scholar on site optimization, provides a great explanation of how site authority works. It's similar to personal networking, only Google is the one watching how the relationships develop.

"I think the way to think about it is like networking in the real world," Odden said. "If you move into a new community and into a new job, a smart person is going to want to establish credibility within this new area or organization, this new sphere of influence. Otherwise, they'll never get anything done or never have any fun with new friends.

"It would make sense for a newcomer to seek out those who already have authority in that neighborhood and create some reason for them to have a conversation and a connection. If that results in an endorsement somehow—like someone invites you to their party or over for dinner—it's a sign to others that you're becoming important in the community too. As a metaphor, that's what Google is looking for—signals of credibility. I don't know that Google actually thinks of things in terms of the content author or not, but there's an expression in information retrieval called 'entities.'

"A known entity can be human, or it can be a company, but it is a thing, like a hub, and it creates content, and it has other entities citing it like blogs and professional journals. These signals are the very origins of Google and the page rank algorithm. Rather than the page rank being associated specifically to a website or web pages, actually, because of the growth of social networks, there are signals of credibility that can identify an individual and follow them wherever they publish.

"If you have a Google+ account, if you have a Google mail account, or a YouTube account, then Google can not only factor in the things it normally looks at like links and content, but it can also look at some of that social stream data and associations.

"And if you write an article on another website like *The Wall Street Journal* or *Fast Company*, your credibility follows you wherever you go because the citation of you and your name comes along with that. This approach harkens back to traditional public relations where if you get positive exposure on other credible sites it could directly help you move your own content because it sends a cumulative signal to Google."

Is there anything you can do to tip the odds in your favor and improve this important rating? Watching SEO professionals duke it out over their best guesses about Google's rating system is a wonderful spectator sport. (It may make a popular Olympic event some day: Google Wrestling.) Even though Google gives us very few clues about the specifics in their formula, remarkably, the SEO authorities are fairly aligned when it comes to the following factors that ultimately result in site authority:

- **The number, quality, and relevance of incoming links** pointing to your content
- **Age of domain:** Older sites have been "in the neighborhood" longer and have had time to become trusted.
- **Size of the website** and the pages of quality information found there
- **The number and quality of outgoing links:** Who do you consider worth linking to? In networking terms, "Who are your friends?" Are they the cool kids who have authority with Google?

- **Indicators of spam:** *Spam* is a broad term indicating unethical, or at least questionable, activities meant to game the system. Do you own 10, 20, or 30 domains that link to each other? Are you pointing to sites known to be spammy? Are you getting lots of links from spammy sites? Google frowns on those practices.

- **Link diversity:** In general, it's better to have a smaller number of links from a wider array of valuable sites than it is to have a large number of incoming links from a handful of sites.

- **Anchor text diversity:** It used to be a good practice to get everyone to link back to your site using the keywords you want to rank on. Google wants to see organic links, and people naturally use different keywords.

- **Speed:** This is becoming increasingly important. If you have a slow website, you'll be penalized in rankings.

- **Temporary versus long-term traffic to the site:** Is a site publishing consistently and getting steady traffic over time? A site that has a sudden spike in traffic may indicate it has purchased traffic, which is frowned upon by Google.

- **The accumulated page value:** On a site with 50 pages, how many of them are valuable?

Traffic metrics like returning visitors, page views per visitor, and time spent on the site can all be increased by working on your Alpha Audience as described in Chapter 5. Google likes to see engagement on your site, known as *dwell time*. If someone finds you on Google, visits your site, and then immediately goes back to Google, it's a good indicator that Google didn't deliver what the customer wanted.

You can begin to see why site authority is the toughest of the six elements of the Content Code to incorporate into a strategy because it takes a lot of hard work and patience! And yet it's too important to ignore.

Since Google doesn't give you any way to quantify the value of your site, independent companies have developed their own ratings which can serve as indicators of performance on search results. One of the leading algorithms is the free Domain Authority tool available on MOZ.com.[1] Their estimate is a logarithmic calculation of the authority of the site, meaning it's easier to rise from score of 30 to 35 than it would be to move from an 80 to 85 (out of a possible 100).

Where do you start with your plan of attack? For that answer, I turn to Ian Cleary, a Dubliner and the founder of Razor Social Media. Ian reliably presents a clear-eyed view of such complex questions.

A plan to improve your authority

According to Cleary, the Domain Authority rating is an accumulation of all the individual rankings of the pages on your site. So if you work on improving individual pages, you'll eventually start moving the domain number up, too.

Page Authority can be improved primarily by increasing the relevant links to your site from pages that have high Page Authority themselves. If someone links to you from a page that has a Page Authority of 70—and this is a relevant link, meaning it's in a similar industry—this link will help your Page Authority. In the neighborhood analogy, it shows that people are getting to know you and recommend you.

Here's an explanation from Google: "Page Authority relies on the uniquely democratic nature of the web by using its vast link structure as an indicator of an individual page's value. In essence, Google interprets a link from page A to page B as a vote, by page A, for page B."

The value of the links depends on the Domain Authority, relevance of the links, and a whole range of other factors. For example, if you're one of 100 links on that page, this link is less beneficial to you than if you were the only link on that page! It can get quite complex, but in summary, if you're looking to get links, it's best if they're from relevant sites with a high Domain Authority, and from pages with a high Page Authority.

When you consistently create content that is interesting and relevant to your niche, build shareability into your content, and develop an Alpha Audience who will ignite your content, you'll inevitably increase your Page Authority. People reference great content and build on ideas all the time, so you'll get links that provide credibility to you by association—you've been "invited to the party." In a very real way, consistently working on the other five elements of the Content Code should eventually raise your Google view. In addition, keep these ideas in mind as you develop content over time:

Exceptional quality encourages conversation. This is why having a blog is important for many businesses that depend on Google search—every blog post represents a new page for Google to index. Each new entry also increases the possibility of new links to your content, which contribute to the authority of your site overall.

Have a link-building strategy. This is art as much as science! Of course, you should aim to get links from high authority sites, but a range of links from both high and low authority sites/pages looks more natural from Google's perspective. An entire industry has been built on providing link-building strategies, and that level of detail is beyond the scope of this book. Here's a sampling of some common ways to earn links:

- **Friends help friends:** Identify key influencers in your industry and get to know them. Find ways to help them and to get on their radar screen. Over time, it's likely they'll link back to you and your familiar content.
- **Link from high authority pages to lower ones:** If you have a high authority page on your site, linking from this page to one with a lower authority on your same site gives it a little boost.
- **Actively seek out links:** Although this is a time-consuming task, it does work. Promote your content to sites that would have a good reason to link to your content. If they don't know of your content, they'll never link to it! One of the best strategies is to identify either the market leader or the nearest competitor (if you're the leader) and look at them in Open Site Explorer. This will tell you where they're getting their links, and then you can go and pitch those folks. It's a nearly foolproof strategy.

Aim for stability. Every time you make structural changes to your site, especially if you start re-naming pages, it could potentially break important internal and external links. This of course destroys these link "friendships" and sends danger signs to Google. If you go through a significant web redesign, work with your developer to make sure authority from existing content gets properly reassigned to the new pages.

Page Authority is not something to obsess about. There is no shortcut to developing this element of the Content Code. It takes years of experience and doing things well online to reach an elite level. But I assure you that if you follow the best practices in this book—even if you do a little each week—your site authority will improve over time.

It's a simple, unified idea. Create exceptional content and then ignite it. If it ignites, the awareness for your content increases. The respect for your content builds. The audience who cares for you magnifies. And you will be welcomed, and maybe even loved, in your new neighborhood.

Side-stepping domain authority

If you don't have the resources to make Domain Authority a priority for your company, you can reframe the issue and approach the problem in a different way. Instead of thinking about it as, "How do I get the content on my website to beat the big sites and show up in my customer search results?" consider it from the perspective, "How do I get my content in front of customers any way I can?"

Here are a few strategies to think about:

- **Curation:** I subscribe to a number of helpful daily, weekly, and monthly newsletters that summarize the best articles in my fields of interest: marketing, entrepreneurship, technology, and design. These newsletters will never show up in Google search results, and yet they're a trusted, consistent source of information delivered in a user-friendly format. Not only do I read the newsletters faithfully, but these curated publications are a primary source of the interesting content I love to share with my audience.

- **LinkedIn:** If you do a search for nearly any B2B company or business-related topic, it's likely that one of the top search results will come from LinkedIn. Perhaps to have an effective search result, you don't need the most powerful website according to Google, but rather you have to have the best content according to LinkedIn. LinkedIn has transformed into the world's largest publisher of business information, and content that is highly-indexed by Google.

- **Groups of influence:** In every industry there are normally small pockets of online influence where thought leaders hang out. It could be a Facebook or LinkedIn Group, a private forum sponsored by one company, or even a close-knit blog community. Becoming active and trusted in these groups can lead to content transmission, and even new Alpha Audience members. How do you find these groups? Ask. Approach leaders in your industry with this query: "I'm trying to learn the ropes in this industry. Could you please recommend online forums, groups, and sources of information that are helpful to you?"

- **Judicious outreach:** Influencers are information junkies and love having the inside scoop first. In fact, they've probably arranged their lives to collect information about the things they're passionate about so they're poised to be the first to share at all times! New information, and especially exclusive information, is like ignition crack to them. I must admit … I am in this category. When somebody who knows me well takes the time to send me a link to an article "they think I will like," it's almost guaranteed that I will read it carefully and share it. Do you have customers like that? Trusted members of your Alpha Audience?

- **Be the hub:** Marketing Consultant Rachel Strella[2] offers this idea for content ignition: "While most are trying to edge their way into a crowded space, I often wonder if it makes more sense to BE the space. This is an idea we proposed to a client in an oversaturated market of government contractors searching for candidates with high levels of security clearance. Until he consulted with us, he was working his way into hundreds of groups, forums, and pages dedicated to military personnel. With competition so fierce, he wasn't sure if working these social media networks was worth the effort. We had to look beyond the common approaches followed by all of his competitors. We spent countless hours of research through social media monitoring to determine the needs of this valuable target audience, which helped guide our content plan. It also gave us the idea to establish strategic content partnerships with a unique non-profit focused mission, and have him create his own 'hub'—an original source of information that can be shared by the community he creates. The idea is that by filling a gap and stepping up to be the voice of authority, his value-based content and community-focused mindset will help him overcome the information density in his niche."

Congratulations! You've unlocked the secrets of the Content Code! But we're not quite finished. Let's examine some ideas for putting this all together and what might happen next on the content marketing scene.

CHAPTER ELEVEN

The Future of Content and Ignition

"When you're finished changing, you're finished."
– Benjamin Franklin

T his is the last chapter of the book, and before we part ways (sniff), we need to figure out what to do with all these ideas. How do you incorporate them practically into your team? And what's on the horizon for your content and ignition?

First things first: Let's get organized.

The ignition department?

If your business has dedicated resources for content creation and social media management, you need to begin thinking about creating a core competency in content ignition as well. What would be the incremental value to your business if you handed a talented employee this book and said "learn it and do this every day?" What would be the business impact if you had a company ignition specialist who drove rapidly increasing levels of content transmission?

This idea of a *content transmission specialist* is already starting to catch on. A pioneer in this field is Brian Lutz, a marketing executive with CBL Properties, who has hired resources specifically for Content Code activities.

"In the last few years, our organic reach on social channels declined due to the increasing number of users per platform, levels of content, and new pay-to-play models, most noticeably at Facebook," Lutz said. "To remain visible on our consumers' timelines, we evolved our content marketing strategy to create content that 'catches fire,' or ignites. We made the decision to hire two Communication Specialists tasked specifically to build shareability into our content. The people in these new roles are special, for two very specific reasons: 1) They've grown up with social media and understand how brands need to communicate and network; and 2) They have excellent analytical skills so they can understand the reasons a particular post or conversation ignites.

"We task our 'Content Ignitors' to focus on all aspects of our business to include outbound conversations in sales, marketing, customer service, and competition monitoring. Since bringing them on board, our content engagement has increased 251 percent year-over-year."

The ignition game plan

Early in this book I emphasized that there's no cookie-cutter content strategy. My hope is that I've introduced enough relevant ideas that some are beginning to become the seeds of a strategy that's right for your organization. Perhaps you have taken notes or highlighted sections of the book. Let's start putting this BADASS concept into action.

The longest chapters in this book were devoted to building shareability into your content and connecting to your Alpha Audience, and for good reason. If you're feeling overwhelmed about where to go from here, these are the two areas worth thinking about first.

As you consider your priorities for a content ignition plan, develop a checklist of daily, weekly, and monthly activities that will lead to greater social transmission over time. This will keep you focused, on-track, and marching steadily toward increased business value from your content investment. A **daily content checklist** for optimizing content transmission might include:

- Maintaining a comprehensive list of possible sites to promote the post. Be judicious. Promote in places best suited for the content and don't drink from the same well too often.
- Creating proactive connections to people and businesses mentioned in your content.
- Monitoring Alpha Audience activities. Look for opportunities to connect with them, serve them, and celebrate their achievements on social platforms.
- Optimizing headlines following the guidelines in this book.

- Finding ways to build optimism, inspiration, and helpful advice into your content.
- Looking for opportunities to embed known "shareability" advantages from Chapters 3 and 4 into every piece of content.
- Making sure your content follows SEO basics.
- Pitching content to appropriate industry syndication sites.
- If appropriate, submitting content to sites like Reddit and StumbleUpon.
- Considering the possible advertising strategy for each post.
- Determining if content could be shared through employee networks.
- Working on short-term strategies to boost social proof.
- Connecting with friends of the business who might appreciate knowing about your content.

Examples of **weekly ignition activities** might include:

- Arranging phone calls and meetings to build relationships with online influencers.
- Organizing specific outreach activities to nurture new members of your Alpha Audience.
- Visiting and promoting Alpha Audience and Influencer content sites.
- Queuing evergreen content for future distribution.
- Developing graphic treatments for upcoming content.
- Creating regular schedules for repurposing existing content.

- Participating in Triberr and other social sharing "clubs" that can introduce your content to relevant new audiences.
- Reaching out to bloggers who publish roundups and letting them know of relevant content.

Monthly ignition activities could include:

- Researching possible new influencers. Create an influencer database for your business.
- Evaluating new distribution platforms, social media groups, and niche bookmarking sites.
- Testing advertising options and strategies.
- Creating long-term plans for repurposing content.
- Looking at appropriate meetings and conference ahead that might be good places to meet customers and build your Heroic Brand.
- Attending conferences that could enhance your personal or business brand and enable connection with Alpha Audience members.
- Considering organizational changes that can help place a focus on content ignition. Are there enthusiastic employees who would want to help you?
- Researching link-building and other long-term strategies that lead to better Site Authority.
- Looking ahead to seasonal opportunities and beginning to work on appropriate content plans.
- Developing content plans that feature a variety of hygiene, hub, and hero content.

These are just a few of the ideas you can begin working on now. Start developing your plan today and put the Content Code to use!

Content ignition and implications for business strategy

When I was starting out in business, my company required me to produce a five-year sales strategy every year. What you see how fast business changes today, that sort of long-term planning seems useless, doesn't it? Undoubtedly, the pace of change is going to increase even more and instead of looking at strategy planning as an obstacle you have to overcome every year, I'd like you to think about your marketing and ignition strategy as a continuous process.

A more useful model for your content strategy might be represented by an American football game. In that sport, a primary method of advancing down the field is to hand the ball to a strong and swift player called a running back. The idea is to create a "hole" in the defense so the running back can take advantage of the opportunity to sprint through a pack of opponents and pick up as much ground as possible before the competition eventually swarms and stops the advance.

Before the game, the team has an over-arching vision of what needs to be accomplished to win, but adjustments are made continually throughout the game. In fact, after each play, the team regroups to consider where another hole might be created. Their strategy flows.

This is how you need to think about business strategy today. As long as you're in the game, you need to be looking for holes, or points of strategic leverage. You need to charge through those holes as fast as you can and gain ground until the competition figures it out and closes in on you, whether that's a few months or a few years.

Meanwhile ... even as this is happening ... you need to be looking for the next hole, the next point of leverage. Plotting a strategy becomes a continuous flow as new research, new platforms, new ignition opportunities, and new content forms create opportunistic points of leverage. Like the running back charging through a hole, your successful strategy is multidimensional, a function of:

- **Space:** What is the point of strategic leverage?
- **Time:** How long will the space (or niche) exist?
- **Speed:** How fast can you run though the gap and maintain the pace ahead of your competitors?
- **Strength:** What special talents do you need on our team to take advantage of the gaps you find?

In an ideal world, a strategic committee would review these dimensions constantly and revise as needed, depending on the structure of the business.

We're at the end of the book and I want to conclude by looking into the future. Here are four final thoughts on where you might take the Content Code next.

Igniting content offline

One of the greatest challenges marketers face is that most of the time, even when we do a great job igniting our content, we don't even know it's happening.

Several research studies[1] show that 70 percent of the content sharing going on in the world is taking place on so-called "dark social" channels such as email, text messaging, or other private, peer-to-peer platforms. It's impossible to see and monitor these channels compared to public social networks such as Facebook, Twitter, Instagram, and Pinterest. About one-third of all people share content *only* on dark channels, meaning the activity of these fans is virtually undetectable.

People tend to share different types of information through light and dark social channels. Consumers generally share politically correct or socially acceptable content in light social channels but share important content such as financial news and political opinions via dark channels.

But there is another form of transmission we haven't covered that is also quite important—word-of-mouth discussions and recommendations. So far, we've only looked at online social transmission. What percent of all word-of-mouth transmission occurs online? 50 percent? 60 percent? Maybe even higher than that?

The actual number is 7 percent according to a study by Keller Fay Group.[2] We tend to overestimate this number because the online version of word-of-mouth transmission is so easy to see and record for measurement purposes. Social media provides such an intoxicating database of tweets, mentions, and posts that it's easy to rely too heavily on these symbols of content transmission.

One could argue (and I am!) that with the evaporation of organic transmission on social media sites, turning your attention to good old offline word-of-mouth marketing may ultimately be the killer app to overcome Content Shock.

If offline ignition is so important, this raises a tantalizing proposition … is there any way you can use some of the principles in this book to carry your content beyond the borders of the social web? Can you use technology in clever ways to enable person-to-person transmission at work, at home, at school, and with friends over dinner?

I think connecting the world of online content and offline word-of-mouth is an area incredibly ripe for innovation.[3]

New analytic tools to uncover Gray Social Media

Somewhere between dark social media lurkers and your "light" social media followers is a third category that is rich in undiscovered marketing opportunity — Gray Social Media. These are the small, still voices who are clearly telling us they're there, but we can't detect their quiet signals and capture the data.

Most current analytics programs are optimized to give us broad trends, patterns, and large-scale shifts in sentiment. But these tools might be missing infrequent messages from people who are quietly telling us "Look at me. I'm in your Alpha Audience!"

Perhaps much of our dark social media really isn't that dark because we're just not looking for their uncommon signals, or we're focused in the wrong places. Innovation and insight don't come from Big Data. They come from Little Data.

Avtar Ram Singh, a digital marketing manager based in Singapore, gave an example of the opportunity of gray social media:

> After working on our company blog for a while, I found great value in diving into Google Analytics to see where the traffic was coming from.

I found a little app link in there that I hadn't seen before and noticed that every week, this place would send us between 20-50 visits. Not a lot, but they were consistently coming from this source.

I discovered that this app was an internal team communication tool. So I knew there was some group out there sharing links to my blog in an environment behind a firewall. This is "dark social media" ... but there was also a clue for me to know they were out there.

I did some sleuthing to check if any agencies I knew in the city used this tool. I came up empty until after several weeks, one of them said through a LinkedIn message that they used it.

It turned out this was a group of marketers who are my exact target audience — loving my content! I would have never known unless I had seen this small signal and dug in to investigate. Now that I knew who they were, I was able to form a business relationship with them.

Is it possible to organize "small signal sleuthing" to discover a whole new category of passionate customers? Consider:

- Somebody I didn't know left me an endorsement for "digital marketing" on LinkedIn. This might be the one and only time I hear from this person, their lone small signal to me that they're a fan. What if I could determine that this was no idle act — this person only gives out two endorsements per year. Wouldn't that be meaningful to know?
- What if a woman among your followers only tweets a few times a month. Her level of tweeting is so obscure

that she's invisible on the social analytics radar. But what if you could determine that 25 percent of her tweets were about your company? Isn't that a "gray signal" that this person cares about your content in an extraordinary way?

- What if you knew that there is a person who ONLY comments on your blog? That means something, even if they only comment twice a year.

Chances are, these "gray" messages are not weak signals at all. These may be the equivalent of the vast, shy, silent majority virtually screaming their love for you! These signals from our quiet, yet essential, Gray Social Media audience are beaming to us all the time, but we're missing them because there's no easy process to track, quantify, and develop these subtle leads. Quiet is not irrelevant!

Certainly CRM and marketing automation software are evolving in a way that can help us begin to discover these quiet voices, but there are still a lot of limits. Wouldn't it provide a competitive advantage if you could sift through the babble on the web better than your competitors to find the important Alpha Audience engaging in the gray area of the social web?

The impact of advanced filters on content ignition

I have seen the future, and it's Zite-like.

Zite is a mobile application that "learns" what content I enjoy. It customizes an evolving delivery system based on what it's learning about me. The more I use it and view content through the app, the better it gets. In fact, it's doing such a good job delivering intensely amazing content that it has become addictive. I've already abandoned many other sources of online news and insight.

But this is not an ad for Zite, which is just one of many innovations to help us navigate through our information-dense world. It's merely a call to action to consider the marketing implications of a new wave of radical content filters.

Five years ago when you did a search on Google for the best deal on an automobile or a review of a new car model, you would get similar results ... probably the same results. But over time, Google has made its search results highly tailored to your environment. Where are you? Who are you? Who are your friends? This information has resulted in an ever-tightening bubble of personalized results. The results you would get today are almost certainly different than what I would get looking for the same information in my town.

Zite is an even more extreme example of this idea, as it actually pushes content to you and only you, radically constricting the scope of possible content you see. Let's say you're trying to create content about automobiles that will be discovered organically by a high-potential customer like me. To get through this filter, you don't have to just ignite your content so that it wins the Google race, you may also have to get it through the Zite algorithm ... and all the other Zite competitors crowding into this increasingly important space. Will that require different strategies? Perhaps we won't just be concerned with SEO—we might also need to consider Zite Engine Optimization. :)

This new era of mega-filters will also present a challenge to any organization or brand trying to introduce a new idea or product. Today when I read an online newspaper or news feed, I'm also presented with many alternative content choices. This content might be way out of my normal comfort zone but interesting to me nonetheless. I like reading about new things. I mean, how else would I learn about twerking?

But as information density increases in my busy world, I can see a day when I spend almost all my time with my own personalized filter. I would rarely see things outside my comfort zone because keeping me *in* my comfort zone is exactly what these filters are trying to do! If Zite figures out I'm politically liberal, it probably won't offer an editorial with a conservative viewpoint. That would be a Filter Fail. Every online organization is collecting data about us and determining what we're going to view and hear based on the stereotype they're creating for us.

While there are obvious benefits to this filtering, the diversity of my content stream is also being strangled by every search and social media platform. Interesting implications for how we learn and discover (or not discover) new ideas, no?

Let's push this idea of radical filtering to an even higher level. Apple's Siri presents a particularly interesting type of content filter and a plucky problem for marketers. If you ask Siri a question, you might get a verbal answer, not necessarily a list of attributed, optimized content (and ads) to choose from.

I recently had a chance to see where this kind of precise search is heading when I met some people who work with Watson, IBM's groundbreaking cognitive computing technology. This may be the ultimate filter because it doesn't just tailor *content* for you, it tailors one precise *answer* for you, even if it's highly complex. Watson can process billions of bits of content and solve even the most difficult query in a heartbeat.

When I asked a Watson team member about the importance of content to this breakthrough technology, she paused and said, "It's not just content to us, *it's fuel.*"

What are the implications for content marketing when we're tasked to provide computer fuel instead of merely blog posts and YouTube videos? Will visual and video content even "count" in that kind of environment?

The necessity to adjust content strategies to a cognitive computing environment will be here soon. This change will certainly hasten the demise of marginal content producers and up the game for good ones as precision content becomes a highly prized resource.

The Internet surrounds us like the air that we breathe

Let's bring the Content Code full circle now. In Chapter 1, I described three digital epochs that led us to Content Shock. I hinted that a fourth epoch is before us. It will be an era of explosive marketing creativity and innovation enabled by wearable technology and augmented reality.

The impact of this development on content and content ignition will be profound … perhaps more profound than the Internet itself. The way we learn, discover, connect, and entertain ourselves will be dramatically altered forever.

Imagine a world in which you're untethered from devices and the strength of a Wi-Fi connection. The Internet will surround you like the air that you breathe—a digital layer on top of the "real world" in any place you choose. Every book, every wall—even a package label—will come alive with interactive possibilities.

This will be an era of marketing without boundaries. We'll no longer be constrained by page size or pixels or a media budget. Marketing will be fueled by an emphasis on fun, immersive experiences. Today, our marketing is geared toward helpfulness, toward utility. But that has severe limits. After you help your customers, how do you continue to engage and grow with them on a daily basis? *"Okay, I've bought my car. Thanks for the useful information. See you in five years when I am ready to buy again."*

But there's virtually no limit to a person's desire to have fun. In fact, we would rather play games and have fun more than almost anything. I think the winners in the next revolution will be creating and igniting fun, immersive experiences on a daily basis for their customers. Like every other marketing phase, early adopters will flourish and those late to the game will struggle. Maybe five years from now I'll be writing about "Fun Shock"—we'll be overwhelmed by competing opportunities to interact. "Minority Report" will seem quaint. Perhaps we're boldly heading toward the next FUNtier. (Get it? I couldn't resist having one final bit of fun with you!)

Share content. Change the world.

We're at the end of our Content Code journey. Writing this book has had a profound impact on me. Uncovering the psychology and sociology of sharing content has made me deeply appreciate the gift of this intimate act, the trust people express when they push that publish button, and the incredible opportunities we all have to care for our world and make it a better place by transmitting the best ideas we find.

In my research I came across a short passage[4] by best-selling author Seth Godin that expresses the emotion and opportunity of social sharing better than I ever could:

I have a friend who can always be counted on to have a great book recommendation handy. Another who can not only tell you the best available movies in theatres, but confidently stand behind his recommendations.

And some people are eager to share a link to an article or idea that's worth reading.

Most people, though, hesitate. "What if the other person doesn't like it..."

The fear of being judged is palpable, and the digital trail we leave behind makes it feel more real and more permanent. We live in an ever-changing culture, and that culture is changed precisely by the ideas we engage with and the ones we choose to share.

Sharing an idea you care about is a generous way to change your world for the better.

The culture we will live in next month is a direct result of what people like us share today. The things we share and don't share determine what happens next.

As we move away from the top-down regime of promoted movies, well-shelved books, and all sorts of hype, the recommendation from person to person is now the most powerful way we have to change things.

It takes guts to say, "I read this and you should too." The guts to care enough about our culture (and your friends) to move it forward and to stand for something.

We'll judge you most on whether you care enough to change things.

You've been such a wonderful and attentive reader that I'd like to reach through this page and thank you in person for reading my book. But that would be creepy.

Perhaps the ultimate achievement from this time we have spent together is that you become a member of my Alpha Audience, and I become a member of yours. But that will only happen if I know you're out there.

I hope you'll connect with me and help me ignite the ideas in this book. If you love what you've read, please share your love abundantly.

And best of all, let's try to meet in person one day. Sound far-fetched? It's not. Chances are I'll be in your city someday soon—watch that Twitter stream! Meeting people in the Alpha Audience is the best part of my job.

Thank you so much for reading my book. Stay in touch, won't you?

You've unlocked the Content Code. Now, go forth and *IGNITE!*

References

Chapter One

1. Nielsen Company report "The US Digital Consumer", http://www.nielsen.com/us/en/insights/reports/2014/the-us-digital-consumer-report.html

2. BusinessesGrow.com, http://www.businessesgrow.com/2014/01/06/content-shock/

3. Sass, Erik "Users are Blind to Branded Content on Social Media" Media Post, http://www.mediapost.com/publications/article/243011/consumers-blind-to-branded-content-on-social-med.html?edition=79840

4. Hansford, Brian, "Turning B2B Readers into Revenue" http://www.heinzmarketing.com/2014/02/siriusdecisions-turning-b2b-readers-revenue/

5. The eMarketer report mentioned can be found at http://www.emarketer.com/public_media/docs/emarketer_social_commerce_roundup.pdf

6. To read more about this case study and view the video, go to http://www.businessesgrow.com/2014/02/10/mirabeau-case-study/

Chapter Two

1. Sheridan, Marcus on The Sales Lion Blog, http://www.the saleslion.com/long-take-business-blog-grow-big-success/
2. YouTube "The Creator Playbook for Brands", http://think. storage.googleapis.com/docs/creator-playbook-for-brands_re-search-studies.pdf

Chapter Three

1. Romero, Goluba, Asur and Huberman Paper presented at technical conferences WWW 2011 and ECML-PKDD 2011 called "Influence and Passivity in Social Media."
2. Facebook research cited in Marketo report, "Contagious Content: http://oginenergy.com/sites/default/files/Contagious-Content.pdf
3. Courtesy of *The New York Times:* http://nytmarketing. whites.net/mediakit/pos   .
4. The psychology of sharing, http://nytmarketing.whsites. mediakit/pos
5. IPA Advertising case studies, http://www.ipa.co.uk/Page/ IPA-Effectiveness-Advertising-Case-Studies#.VK1swNE5DlZ
6. Naaman, Boase and Lai "Is it Really About Me?" Proceedings from ACM Conference (2010)
7. Mitchell and Tamir, "Disclosing Information About the Self is Intrinsically Rewarding" Proceeding of the National Academy of Science (2012)
8. Tierney, John, "Good News Beats Bad News on Social Networks" *The New York Times,* http://www.nytimes.com/2013 /03/19/science/good-news-spreads-faster-on-twitter-and-facebook
9. 2011 Journal of Marketing Research, American Marketing Association

10. "Coming Clean on Facebook Reach", http://www.businessesgrow.com/2014/08/25/facebook-reach-2/

11. Maloney, Devon, "Popularity of Quizzes comes from Fear, Not Narcissism" *Wired* http://www.wired.com/2014/03/buzz-feed-quizzes/

Chapter Four

1. Courtesy eConsultancy, https://econsultancy.com/reports/internet-statistics-compendium

2. Study cited here: http://www.7boats.com/generate-more-lead-with-social-sharing/

3. Spool, Jared, "The $300 million button" on User Interface Engineering, http://www.uie.com/articles/three_hund_million_button

4. Courtesy of *The New York Times:* http://nytmarketing.whites.net/mediakit/pos

5. Pew Research Study: http://www.pewresearch.org/fact-tank/2014/02/03/6-new-facts-about-facebook/

6. 2011 Journal of Marketing Research, American Marketing Association

7. This research was reported in a research report by Marketo: http://oginenergy.com/sites/default/files/Contagious-Content.pdf

8. BuzzSumo: http://okdork.com/2014/04/21/why-content-goes-viral-what-analyzing-100-millions-articles-taught-us/

9. Edelstyn, Simon, "5 tips to help you improve your headline click-through rate", http://www.theguardian.com/media-network-outbrain-partner-zone/5-tips-headline-click-through-rate

10. Moon, Garret, "Make your content more shareable with these five tricks" Buffer Blog https://blog.bufferapp.com/shareable-content-social-media-research

11. Medina, John, Statistic from Brain Rules, http://www.brain rules.net/vision

12. Simply Measured study: http://cdn.simplymeasured.com/wpcon tent/uploads/2013/08/SimplyMeasured-Facebook-Study-July-2013.pdf

13. Edelstyn, ibid

14. http://www.businessesgrow.com/2013/04/02/heres-why-100000-people-unfollowed-me-on-twitter/

15. Libert, Kelsey, "Outreach Strategies for more social shares" https://blog.bufferapp.com/outreach-strategies-for-more-social-shares

16. Much of the source material for this section came from a blog post written for the {grow} blog by Kathi Kruse. http://www.businessesgrow.com/2012/02/02/six-ways-to-turn-yelp-into-your-most-effective-marketing-channel/

17. Nielsen blog. http://www.nielsen.com/us/en/insights/news/2013/under-the-influence-consumer-trust-in-advertising.html

18. Kolowich, Lindsay "The Rules of Twitter Hashtags: Hits and Misses From 7 Big Brands, "Hubspot Blog http://blog.hub spot.com/marketing/twitter-hashtag-campaign-examples

19. This case study is adapted from "Why Content Spreads" by Leo Widrich on the Buffer blog https://blog.bufferapp.com/what-makes-content-go-viral-the-anatomy-of-a-post-that-got-over-500000-likes

20. Tierney, John "Good News Beats Bad News on Social Networks" *New York Times* http://www.nytimes.com/2013/03/19/science/good-news-spreads-faster-on-twitter-and-facebook

21. Seiter, Courtney "How Our Brains Decide What to Share Online" *Fast Company* http://www.fastcompany.com/3027699/how-our-brains-decide-what-we-share-online

Chapter Five

1. "The Kid Who Wanted a Door for Christmas" {grow} blog: http://www.businessesgrow.com/2012/11/27/the-kid-who-wanted-a-door-for-christmas/

2. Information and some direct content in this section came from the 2014 report "What Social Media Analytics Can't Tell You About Your Customers" by VisionCritical. The entire report is available here: http://ow.ly/GKxAH

3. Pew Research Social Networking Fact Sheet: http://www.pewinternet.org/fact-sheets/social-networking-fact-sheet/

4. Pew Research report "Millennials will Make Online Sharing a Lifelong Habit." http://www.pewinternet.org/2010/07/09/millennials-will-make-online-sharing-in-networks-a-lifelong-habit/

5. The Edison Research Social Habit study is available at www.edisonresearch.com

6. Think with Google report: https://www.thinkwithgoogle.com/articles/social-engagement-buying-question.html

7. Jeffrey Rohrs quote came from the eBook "Building and Audience Development Strategy for Content Marketing" created by The Content Marketing Institute and TopRank Marketing

8. This GoPro example came from "How to Turn Your Customers into Brand Fans" By Michele Linn http://contentmarketinginstitute.com/2014/10/how-to-turn-customers-brand-fans/

9. The Urban Outfitter and J. Crew case studies appeared in an article called "CPG: Social Reciprocity Can Work For Your Brand, Too" by Liz Aviles that was in the December 2014 Media Post newsletter

10. Case study courtesy Vocus whitepaper "Eight great ways to generate publicity"

11. Citation from J. James: "The Psychological Continuum Model: A Conceptual Framework for Understanding an Individual's Psy-

chological Connection to Sport" www.sciencedirect.com/science/article/pii/S144135230170071

12. Seth Godin's comments first appeared on Seth's Blog "What did the fox say" http://sethgodin.typepad.com/seths_blog/2013/09/what-does-the-fox-say.html

13. The Colman and Stratten quotes in this section came from the eBook "Building and Audience Development Strategy for Content Marketing" created by The Content Marketing Institute and TopRank Marketing

14. Gini Dietrich's comments first appeared on The Social Fresh Blog http://socialfresh.com/how-to-build-community-on-a-blog/

15. Kawasaki, Guy, "Enchantment: The Art of Changing Hearts, Minds, and Actions"

Chapter Six

1. To read the full Groove story, reference https://www.groovehq.com/blog/1000-subscribers

Chapter Seven

1. Many of the themes for this section came from the book *Return On Influence* (McGraw-Hill).

2. Quote first appeared on the Small Business Ideas blog: http://www.smallbusinessideasblog.com/how-to-promote-your-blog

3. Segal, David, "Riding the Hashtag in Social Media Marketing" *New York Times* http://www.nytimes.com/2013/11/03/technology/riding-the-hashtag-in-social-media-marketing

4. "How great leaders inspire action", http://www.ted.com/talks/simon_sinek_how_great_leaders_inspire_action

5. Segal ibid

6. Altucher, James "What I learned about life after interviewing 80 highly successful people" http://www.jamesaltucher.com/2015/

01/what-i-learned-about-life-after-interviewing-80-highly-suc-
cessful-people/

7. Many of the ideas in this section are inspired by the article "How
   to Promote Yourself Without Being a Jerk" by Dorie Clark
   which appeared in *Harvard Business Review* Online: http://ow.ly/
   Gl4Ai

8. *New York Times,* "Your Brain on Fiction" http://www.nytimes.
   com/2012/03/18/opinion/sunday/the-neuroscience-of-your-brain
   -on-fiction.html?_r=1&

9. *Psychology Today,* "How Social Media Inflames Jealousy" by Ira
   Hyman   http://www.psychologytoday.com/blog/mental-
   mishaps/201406/how-social-networks-can-inflame-jealousy

Chapter Eight

1. This case study courtesy of the Vocus white paper "Eight Great
   Ways to Generate Publicity"

2. Courtesy Hubspot: http://blog.hubspot.com/marketing/2013-in
   bound-marketingstats-charts

3. http://www.businessesgrow.com/2014/01/06/content-shock/

4. http://www.businessesgrow.com/2014/06/02/rising-social-media-
   stars/

5. http://www.businessesgrow.com/2014/11/11/speech-will-never-
   hear/

Chapter Nine

1. Jay Baer's quotes on social proof in this chapter originally appeared in my book *"Return On Influence."*

Chapter Ten

1. A host of free rating tools are available on the MOZ site: https://moz.com/researchtools/ose/
2. Strella, Rachel, "4 Ideas to Ignite Your Content", http://strellasocialmedia.com/2015/01/4-ways-ignite-content/

Chapter Eleven

1. Mandese, Joe "Study shed new light on dark social media" Media Post, http://www.mediapost.com/publications/article/239139/study-sheds-new-light-on-dark-social-finds-cons.html
2. Keller, Ed and Fay, Brad The Face-to-Face Book: Why Real Relationships Rule in a Digital Marketplace (2012 Free Press)
3. An excellent article on this topic comes from Ardath Albee: "Extend content reach with B2B buying committees", http://marketinginteractions.typepad.com/marketing_interactions/2014/12/extend-content-reach-with-b2b-buying-committee.html
4. Godin, Seth, "You Are What You Share" http://sethgodin.typepad.com/seths_blog/2015/01/you-are-what-you-share.html

Acknowledgements

This book is a tribute to friends and business professionals who have supported me and this incredible labor of love. For the dozens of people interviewed for this book – the people who MADE this book -- I humbly say thank you. I have the greatest Alpha Audience in the world.

A special woman, Brittany Suzette Shaffer has been my intern for four years. She did absolutely crazy things to help me with the research I needed to pull off something as ambitious as a book on an entirely new subject. Also a hat tip to Don Stanley of the University of Wisconsin for help with some additional research.

Christopher Penn, Bernadette Jiwa, Ian Cleary, Eric Wittlake, and Lee Odden provided feedback and guidance that helped improve the completeness and accuracy of the book.

Sarah Mason is the artistic director for Schaefer Marketing Solutions and is responsible for the handsome cover and interior design of the book. Thanks to Cody Butcher for design guidance on The Content Code cover art.

Elizabeth Rea was the editor for the book and helped keep the writing tight any time I started to get too colloquial!

It takes a special person to live with me when I am immersed in the difficult all-consuming process of writing a book and thank God I have the perfect wife, Rebecca. Thank you my love for your tolerance and cheerfulness in the face of my frenzied creative process.

All my gifts come from God. My prayer is that this book has glorified Him in some small way.

Index

About the Author

Mark W. Schaefer is a globally-recognized blogger, speaker, educator, business consultant, and author who blogs at {grow} — one of the top marketing blogs of the world.

Mark has worked in global sales, PR, and marketing positions for more than 30 years and now provides consulting services as Executive Director of U.S.-based Schaefer Marketing Solutions. He specializes in social media training and clients include both start-ups and global brands such as Dell, Johnson & Johnson, Adidas, and the U.S. Air Force.

Mark has advanced degrees in marketing and organizational development and is a faculty member of the graduate studies program at Rutgers University. A career highlight was studying under Peter Drucker while studying for his MBA.

He is the author of four other best-selling books, *Social Media Explained, Return On Influence, Born to Blog,* and *The Tao of Twitter,* the best-selling book on Twitter in the world. He is among the world's most recognized social media authorities and has been a keynote speaker at many conferences around the world including Social Media Week London, National Economic Development Association, the Institute for International and European Affairs, and Word of Mouth Marketing Summit Tokyo.

You can stay connected with Mark online at www.BusinessesGROW.com and by following his adventures on Twitter: @markwschaefer.

Printed in Great Britain
by Amazon